TABLE OF CONTENTS

In memory of Mae Chu, for trusting me to love
and care for your eldest son Michael.

In memory of Eden Elizabeth, who had to leave
the love of her life Colin far too soon.

This book is dedicated to the legacy that Michael and I have, our children, mine, Andrew and Jeremy, his Alexandra and Eric. Our love for our children knows no boundaries.

I have always wanted to write this book because I feel it is important to share our love story. I began writing it on September 9, 2008, just under a month after Michael died. It has taken so very long as it has been emotional and heart wrenching to write. Many times I have had to stop for months as I would be an emotional wreck.

I first started the book as I needed to have a record of us. I did not want to forget anything. Michael told me he did not want to be forgotten and asked me to prepare dishes from his recipes as a way of keeping him alive.

I believe it is in our nature to want to be remembered, to know that our lives mattered and that we made an impact during our short time in this world.

It is a unique and special story because it is ours. But it is no more special than the millions of love stories in the world and not just those between a man and a woman, but those between two men, two women, a parent and their child, brothers, sisters, aunts, uncles, cousins, friends and any relationship based on love. Love is what makes us human.

Special thanks to the dear people in my life, my family and my friends. My sons Andrew and Jeremy who had to watch their Mom go from so happy to so lost after Michael died. You both kept me going and I am so sorry it was so very tough for you. I am also most grateful for Andrew's partner Steph, who has only been in our family for a few years, but she has been a wonderful support and is dearly cherished.

I am blessed to have three sisters and a brother. I want to thank my sister Tracey for always being more than a sister, but a friend that I can always talk to. Thank you for loving me just the way I am. And to my little sister Nancy, we share a love of music, movies and art. You never hesitate to say "I love you big sis" and give me a hug.

A very special thank you to Michael's parents Dick and Mae Chu who were so amazing despite their pain at slowly losing their son. Mae passed away in January 2014 and I miss her a great deal. She was the mother-in-law I always dreamed of having. As we got to know each other, I came to love her so very much and when she passed away it was much more difficult for me than I ever expected. I was lucky enough to spend an hour with her in the hospital just two days before she died and we had a wonderful talk. She had really understood and supported our relationship.

To Michael's brother Baree Chu and his fiancé, my dear GFIL (girlfriend-in-law) Molly Spencer, I couldn't have survived without you. As well thank you to Mary Anne Chu, the mother of Michael's children for your kindness and friendship.

To the best friends I could ever ask for, Melanie Walker and Jocelan Tracey who helped me get through the toughest time in my life. Your compassion and caring are a blessing in my life and I am so grateful. To my childhood friend Margy, thank you for being there many times over the years.

A very special thank you to Dr. Wendy Kendal for encouraging me to share my story when I told her about it during a very difficult time in my health; you gave me the encouragement I needed and I thank you. You referred me to Jane Goranson-Coleman. From the bottom of my heart, thank you Jane for guiding me through one of the most difficult years in my life. You have helped me to finally heal.

"Some people come into our lives, leave footprints on our heart, and we are never, ever the same." Unknown.

PlentyOfFish website:

Michael wrote "I am new to this site and would love to find the woman I've been looking for all my life, my best friend and lover. I am 2nd generation Canadian with lots of British Columbian family history... You are a non-smoker, honest, sincere, warm and caring with very insignificant issues. I spend my time cherishing every minute of my life, appreciating it's challenges and try to live it to the max as we only have one crack at it."

Cynda wrote "My life is happy but I am at the point where I am wanting to find someone special to share it with. I know who I am and what I want. I am emotionally and financially stable. I am looking for a like minded person. Someone who wants to make a difference in life. Someone who wants to be healthy and fit or is striving to be. We all had to start somewhere. I don't play head games, life is too short for that. I want someone who is honest, has integrity, is sincere and most of all, down to earth."

For Michael,
Love Cynda

It, life that is, is a constantly changing process. Some days I wake up feeling pretty good, and others the thought hits me as soon as I wake up. My Michael is gone. He's dead and there is nothing I can do to change the situation. I can't bring him back. There is no rewind on life.

I feel the overwhelming urge to throw up, give up and just lie there in a heap of tears. I know I can't, as they say life does go on and mine has continued to do so in this past year. I have had to make myself go on. Losing (what a silly expression as I didn't misplace him but he is no longer physically here on this earth with me) him has been the hardest thing I have ever dealt with in my life, yet it has also been the most life changing experience ever. To this day I would never trade my time with Michael for a safe, comfortable life.

At times he told me how I saved his life, but in reality he saved mine. Something was always missing before I met him and he filled that void. The intensity of the pain of living without him continues to lessen over time and the joy of having been so very loved replaces that space more and more as time goes on.

You won't get flowery prose from me. Life is tough and this whole experience has rocked my world, good and bad. Some days it's hell but other days I laugh a little harder, smile a bit brighter and I know that I am going to be okay. They say that grieving has its peaks and valleys. Special dates and holidays trigger memories as do rituals, songs, places and anything in life that you shared together. I am the crazy Asian lady walking around the grocery store trying not to burst into tears as I pick up a green onion because I remember how Michael wouldn't buy green onions unless he could get the same discount for buying one that you would only get when you bought two.

After finding, loving and being loved by Michael, I really do now believe my life was planned out from the very beginning.

Please let me share with you the story of the love of my life, Michael.

CHAPTER ONE
PLENTY OF FISH

January 11, 2007

This was the day that would change my life forever.
On January 7th I went to the PlentyOfFish website to
find a nice Chinese man. I wanted a nice Chinese man
because I had been out on three dates with a Caucasian
man that I was convinced was planning to cheat on his
wife with me.

When you look at the site, you can see when the person
was last online. The man I had dated had been online
pretty much every night since I had met him. I decided
that I would go to the other end of the spectrum and
look for a man that was not "trolling" as I put it.

Michael was that man. I found him at the other end and
he looked like a nice man. He had some pictures with
his adult children and he had a nice profile. The only
thing that was of any concern for me was that he wrote
that his religion was other. My first thought was I
hope he is not a Jehovah's Witness. No disrespect to
those of that faith, it just isn't for me. If he was,
it won't work.

I sent him an email and he sent me the following response:

*Thank you for your reply. I would be glad to speak
with you. Like I have always said, you can never have
enough friends.*

*Call me if you like at 778-555-6907 or email mchu7@telus.
net or fred_flounder@hotmail.com for messenger. I am a
bit of a nitehawk so don't worry if it's too late.*

Michael

Home 604-555-1960

I called him on Thursday night, January 11, 2007. I
had taken my teenage son Jeremy to the walk in medical
clinic as he had a sore throat and we didn't get back
home until about 9:30ish. Michael's voice was warm
and resonated pleasantly. He was very easy to talk to
and we talked for two hours. We would have talked all
night if I didn't have to get up for work. The conversation flowed naturally.

He went over what he had posted on his profile on the
PlentyOfFish dating site. He started to tell me that
his family was from Lillooet. I told him that my Aunty
Elaine and Uncle Stan were from Lytton and that my
uncle was born there. He said that he knew Stan Lee
but it turned out it was a different Stan Lee. We
later found out that his Mom knew my Aunty Elaine and
had gone to Sunday school with her.

I did call up Aunty Elaine to get the scoop on the
family. I just wanted to confirm that Michael was
really who he said he was. I was going to be careful
and protect myself.

He asked me how tall I was. I told him 5 feet. He
liked that, as he was 5'5". I always preferred tall

guys but always ended up with ones that weren't more than 5'6".

During this phone conversation he told me that he was terminally ill with cancer. He said it was stage 4 and he told me the form of lung cancer that he had. He was honest and up front. He told me about the treatment that he had had so far and where his cancer currently stood. He wasn't in remission but it was currently under control.

He was also a Type 2 diabetic and his diabetes was managed with insulin and additional medication. He told me about his diabetes later on.

He gave me the chance to back out now, before we would ever meet. I had no intention of backing out. In my entire life I had never talked to a man who intrigued and interested more. I only hoped that he wanted to meet me as much and that our date would happen.

I could and should have been scared at the prospect, and run like hell the other way but I didn't. All I knew was that I could not wait to meet him. If nothing more came of this date, this was a man I wanted to be friends with. To me he was an incredibly brave man.

There was a comfortableness right from the very beginning. We began to communicate by email right after we spoke.

Our first date was to happen on Saturday, January 20, 2007. He was getting back from his Palm Springs golf trip on Friday, January 19th and said he would call me then and make arrangements. I was anxious about him calling and just a bit scared that he wouldn't.

That Friday, after work, I had a glass of wine with my co-workers but didn't stay too long as I wanted to get home to receive Michael's phone call. (I was employed as a Legal Secretary at Stikeman Elliott LLP, a prestigious law firm with locations all over the world. I had been a Legal Secretary since 1993.) I only needed a glass or two of wine to be tipsy and I really didn't want to make the wrong impression on Michael.

January 19, 2007

He called me on the Friday night as promised. We talked about dinner plans and he said that I should pick wherever I wanted to go. It didn't matter where he said, dinner was on him. I decided to choose Osamu Sushi Japanese Restaurant, a sushi restaurant with Japanese sushi chefs that my sister Abby had talked about. I had never been there and I thought it would be a good place to go. I told Michael I would make reservations and he joked about having a secretary and said he liked that.

He insisted on coming to pick me up and we settled on a time.

CHAPTER TWO
FIRST DATE

January 20, 2007

First date night. I wanted dinner to be perfect, to look just right, and God forbid not throw up at dinner. I was nervous, really nervous but also really excited. I carefully planned my time to get ready. I showered and took care with styling my hair just right, and choosing what to wear. I was very fit, exercised almost daily and knew that I looked really good. As I was blow drying my hair, Michael called to say he was running late. He ended up being about 15 minutes late. I later found out that he was often late and I would tease him about being late for our first date.

I answered my door and there he was...the most adorable man. He probably wasn't so fond of my description but that's how he looked to me. He was wearing his favourite pink and okay, for the colour challenged guys, salmon coloured shirt and a nice car coat. He looked exactly like his picture. He was grinning from ear to ear and he immediately made me feel special. He commented that wow I looked exactly like my picture. I wore a brown jersey knit dress that showed off my hard worked for figure, brown stilettos, a red narrow knit scarf and a red leather jacket. There was no way

I was ever going to lie about how I looked or who I am on a dating site as I wanted more than just a first date. I was honest on my profile and if the guy didn't like it, next…!

He teased me about how hard it was to find my townhouse based on my vague description of being behind a big tree. I did give him the parking spot number as that made it easier to find my home.

He drove an older BMW, four door sedan and like a gentleman, he opened the car door for me. He waited while I got in and closed the door for me. The weather cooperated and it was a pleasant and dry evening and the drive to the restaurant was nice. We talked all the way. He was very candid and immediately told me about his special muffins and how he had baked some and had one while golfing that really threw him for a loop. We had good laughs over that. He opened himself up to me right away and it was really a case of what you see is what you get.

The restaurant was cozy and had a nice ambiance. I had reserved a tatami room as I wanted privacy so we could really talk. We sat on opposite sides of the table. In time, on future dates, we often sat next to each other.

We had sashimi, wakame seaweed salad and sushi. The sushi was beautifully presented, very fresh and tasty. Rice was done just right and everything was superb. Perhaps, part of it was the company as well.

Michael ordered everything. It was so nice to be out with a man that was comfortable with himself and knew what he wanted. I was happy to let him take care of everything. I wasn't used to this, I often made the decisions and this was a nice change for me. For a first date it was quite an intimate dinner and I guess in some ways, it was almost a second date as our first conversation on the phone was more like a coffee date. He showed me a lot of pictures off of his camera, his recent golf trip and pictures of many of his family members.

We talked a great deal and I told him I had a few tattoos and pointed to where they were. He was intrigued by this and later on he told me that he used to have this attitude about tattoos, but after he got cancer, tattoos were not a big deal to him.

We never went back to this restaurant again although we really enjoyed it. Maybe it was just more special as our first date restaurant, I am not sure. As well, there were too many other places in other locations that have been more convenient.

We left the restaurant around 11 pm as I was working the next day for another lawyer to earn "grocery money". I had two sons to feed and the eldest Andrew was always starving or way too full.

He brought me home and I invited him in and quickly showed him my living room and a few pictures on the wall and then he gave me a quick kiss and left. I cleaned my living room earlier that day, just in case.

> *From: Cynda*
> *To: Michael*
> *Date: Sunday, January 21, 2007 7:54 PM*
> *Subject: Last Night*

Dear Michael:

Just hanging out watching tv with Jeremy and sitting here in my pink slippers and Snoopy jammies. I guess that makes me sound Asian. I do have what Andrew calls "Honger" jammies. The slippers are boots though, lined with fur.

Thought I would send you an email in case you are out or busy. I just wanted to thank you again for such a lovely evening. You are a funny, intelligent, articulate and gentle guy. I had a really good time.

You shared so much with me that I feel like I have known you for a long time. I am touched that you were so candid.

I don't know what your schedule is but I had a thought:

If you are available and interested, you could put on your best power suit and meet me at Park Place this Friday, the 26th. I can show you Stikeman and then we could go for lunch at the Wedgewood Hotel or anywhere else you would like to go to. I would be pleased to treat you and after lunch we could perhaps go for a walk in the West End and I can show you where I grew up. I can take the afternoon off work.

You are a special and brave man. I want you to know that I really would like to be part of your life. Your honesty about your cancer scares the crap out of me but I truly believe you are going to win your fight and I would like to be there for you.

BTW, glad you kissed me. Anyways, life is short and I don't want to waste time by not saying how I feel. I am old-fashioned but with a twist and a dash of spice.

For Michael, Love Cynda

I really believe that everyone that comes into a person's life does so for a reason.

Cynda

I will be up tonite till 10. If you want to call, after 9 is good.

Michael told me that we didn't have to do anything that fancy as I suggested in the email as it wasn't really him.

Later in the week he called and asked if I wanted to go for Dim Sum on Saturday. I told him that I wasn't available during the day as I had plans to exercise and do grocery shopping with my sister Abby, but that I was free in the evening. He said he would plan something.

From: Michael
To: Cynda
Date: Friday, January 26, 2007 5:19 PM
Subject: Re: Hello

Hi, Thank you so much for the beautiful day. Maybe you will pick this note up after your run if you check your work station out before you leave tonite. I am assuming your running down there in the west end somewhere.
I'm starting to feel better each day, although a bit bored here by myself and what tv I can hack. Been reading a bit. Went over to Pine Valley Golf course and putted a bit. Couldn't last long, a bit chilly.
Something warm and some cuddles would be nice.
Any way , will give you a call this eve to see how things are and whats going to go on tomorrow.
Michael

January 26, 2007

It was after work and I had just left the office to go for a run. I was running across Pender Street and just passing the Starbucks, heading towards the water when Michael called.

To this day, I cannot pass that corner without thinking about him. I have often cried when I run that route. I can remember so clearly the phone ringing, hearing his voice, and how thrilled I was to be talking to him again.

He told me he bought some tickets from someone in a parking lot for Colin James who was playing on Saturday. I had never seen Colin James perform before but knew of him and Michael was a big fan.

I invited Michael to dinner at my place before the concert and I made udon soup and some gyozas. We left for the concert, arrived downtown, parked and then went for coffee and tea. I have always been fond of rings and wore several on each hand. Michael was intrigued by all of them and asked me about each ring. He was an attentive listener and always remembered everything I told him.

Before the concert started, we continued to talk, about my older son Andrew's schooling as he was currently away at Nichols College, located in Dudley, Massachusetts, about an hour's drive from Boston.

The concert was wonderful and we enjoyed it immensely. Michael kept smiling at me and grabbing my knee and squeezing it. He was also coughing quite a bit and told me not to be concerned. I was so crazy about this man that I just wanted him to hold me tight and never let go. I had only just met him and already I had such strong feelings for him.

> *From: Michael*
> *To: Cynda*
> *Date: Sunday, January 28, 2007 12:33 PM*
> *Subject: Little Big Band Nite*
>
> *Hi Cynda,*
>
> *Just a note to thank you for such a lovely evening last nite. I really enjoyed dinner last nite, in fact it would rival any "go out" dinner anytime. You've found one of my major weaknesses. Oh no. ....Wasn't Colin James fantastic ?*
>
> *I'm so sorry, but Tuesday has been consumed with daughter and son. My daughter called today and wanted to come over. Wednesday could be a possibility, no promises though. I will be talking to you soon. Have a great day !*
>
> *Michael*
>
> *PS: How are you at just cuddling around a video at home?*
>
> *From: Cynda*
> *To: Michael*
> *Date: Monday, January 29, 2007 9:40 AM*
> *Subject: RE: Little Big Band Nite*
>
> *Michael:*
>
> *Thanks for your first nice note and this one too. I usually turn my computer off as soon as I leave the office so unfortunately I didn't get to read it till now.*
>
> *...*
> *I had a wonderful time with you on Saturday. The evening was perfect.*

So glad you enjoyed dinner. It was my pleasure.

I like picnics and we can plan for that some time soon.

I will call you tonite around 9 if that works for you.
Cuddling and a video sounds great since you are so good
at cuddling.

Cynda

January 30, 2007

Today Michael had an appointment at the BC Cancer Agency Clinic for tests.

Right from the very beginning Michael was always an open book and honest with me. I found it incredibly refreshing and it made him that much more attractive to me. He had such passion for life, great love for his children, family, and friends. He also respected and loved the mother of his children, Mary Anne. This was important to me as I would always love the father of my eldest, Kimbo and he would always be a part of my life.

January 31, 2007

After work, I came over to his place for the first time and we just hung out and talked. He told me that he wasn't sure if it would be a good idea to get involved as he was concerned about me. I told him that I am a big girl and I can handle it. As we got to know each other more and discovered so many connections, we came to believe that our meeting was inevitable.

I didn't say anything about the looks of his apartment at first and he hassled me about this later that day. As I started to spend more time there, he bought cushions for the sofa, cleaned out a dresser drawer and made closet space for me. He did everything he could to make his home mine as well. It was all new for me and very sweet. I was dating a grownup.

Michael was interested in compatibility based on the Chinese Horoscope and he made some comments about whether we would be compatible or not. I was born in the year of the Ox and he in the year of the Horse. He did some research and it turned out we had a compatibility rating of 5 out of 10. Since we both liked to gamble, we seemed to be a good bet.

February 1, 2007

Michael was going to Las Vegas for a few days on a trip that was previously planned. He would be going to see Elton John and doing a bit of gambling.

> *From: Michael*
> *To: Cynda*
> *Date: Thursday, February 1, 2007 12:40 AM*
> *Subject: yes I think about ya a lot*
>
> *Hi there,*
> *Happy anniversary at work. Hope its a nice day for you today. How was the sleep in?*
> *Well I managed to navigate home safely last nite as you may have well guessed.*
> *Thank you so much for the cookies, I love em, yummm-mmm. And thanks for a nice evening too.*
> *Anyway, enjoy superbowl day and I'll try to ring u (perhaps on cell) if I get a chance. Packing this morning, so have a great day. I'll try to win us a trip!*
> *Michael.*

From: Cynda
To: Michael
Date: Thursday, February 1, 2007 10:26 AM
Subject: RE: yes I think about ya a lot

Morning Michael:

It has been a good day so far. It was nice to have a later, slower morning. I didn't really sleep in as I guess my body is so used to getting up early. Watched a little Gilmore Girls that I taped from Tuesday while getting ready to go to work.

Very glad you got home safely as that was pretty thick fog. I figured though, that the worst of the Chinese Richmond drivers were not out and about.

I had another wonderful evening with you and when I say I will miss you it is because I have gotten accustomed to talking, emailing and seeing you.

Good luck gambling. I bought a lotto ticket this am too. As they say, you never know.

Talk to u soon. If you can't reach me on the cell on Sunday try me at home as I don't think I'll be later than 9.

Cynda

BTW, really like the subject line. I think about you often and sometimes it is a little distracting.

From: Michael
To: Cynda
Date: Thursday, February 1, 2007 11:16 AM
Subject: RE: yes I think about ya a lot

...

*Have a great day and the next few days. I'm having
breakfast at the little Italian nook at Bellagio tomorrow.
Homemade granola and muffins, best coffee and breakfast
in all of Vegas.*
Ciao Bella,
Michael

February 3, 2007

I was out for Saturday morning exercise with my
sisters Abby and Harriet, when Michael surprised me
with a phone call from Las Vegas. I was so happy to
hear his voice and it meant a lot that he was calling
me when he was on vacation.

February 5, 2007

He gave me his return flight time and I called him as
soon as his plane landed; literally, as he had not yet
gotten off the plane. I had really missed him.

This trip to Las Vegas had been planned before I met
Michael and he was going with a female friend. She was
a former co-worker who he had known for many years. He
told me that she was most unhappy that I was in his
life. A few months before meeting me he dated another
woman but she ended it after a few dates as his cancer
diagnosis was more than she could deal with.

The things happened with his female friend were a bit unnerving. He told
me that she was angry when he called me from Las Vegas and she was
angry again when I called him just as the plane landed. She called my
home once but I never answered the phone.

Later on I was in a running race and her pace coincidentally was very
similar to mine so she was running just behind me. Another time she
went to visit Michael at the apartment and there was a lovely potted

arrangement of daffodils and other spring flowers. She found out they were from me and she mangled the flowers with her hands.

I was clear with Michael from the onset. I of course expected that there were other women in his life before me and that I am very new in his life at this point. I could leave now before getting further involved. I had no wish to become entangled in something and get hurt. I told him it was his decision. He said he did not want to lose the friendship with her but he was not going to give me up as I made him happy.

I told him that I had no issue if he wanted to continue his friendship with her and he continued to have some contact throughout his illness. I was never involved, nor did she ever contact me again. I had told him after she phoned me that I would not hesitate to contact the police if she ever contacted me or my children.

There was sporadic contact up until his death and I know that he missed her friendship.

February 7, 2007

I went to Michael's place after work and I told him that I would bring dinner. I picked up some paninis and a chocolate pear tart baked by Thomas Haas for us to share for dessert.

After dinner we just sat around, cuddled, kissed and talked. I felt very content and happy. It all felt just right. We listened to Kenny Chesney and Michael played his piano for me.

Michael told me that although the paninis were really delicious, he didn't really like having sandwiches for dinner, as sandwiches are a lunch item. Food was very important to Michael and he had strong opinions about food amongst other things. He thoroughly enjoyed the pear tart and I think I scored a few points for my dessert choice. Paninis were quickly forgotten.

February 8, 2007

I am not sure when it happened but it was almost from the beginning. When we weren't together we started to have nightly phone conversations before bed. They were always lengthy and we really got to know each other. I cherished those phone calls as they were so special.

We talked about our upcoming weekend together and we had telephone confessions. Michael told me he had false teeth and I told him I had a piercing. He liked that and was looking forward to seeing it.

We soon had nicknames for each other as well. I have always liked the name Fred, as I am very fond of Fred Flintstone but more importantly a huge fan of Freddie Mercury. As fishing was one of Michael's great passions he used the email names "Jake Trout" and "Fred Flounder". I joked that with a Chinese accent I would call him "Flet" instead of "Fred". He soon became either "Mr. Flet", "Big Flet" or "BF". His nicknames for me were "Sweetee", "Glamour Pussy" or "GP" and also Honey Pot Pie or "HPP".

In this fast paced world, everything happens so fast that sometimes you never get to anticipate something as it is just there. The anticipation of spending our first night together, the romance, the mystery and newness was special. I was grateful that even though we had both been married and divorced, that we were not so cynical that we could not find such joy in the anticipation of what was to come.

Cynda Yeasting

February 9, 2007

This was my last day working for the lawyer John at his home office as I had decided that I wanted to spend all my spare time with Michael. I went in on the Friday after my day job so that I could avoid tying up my time on the weekend. Michael wanted to come pick me up after work and drive me home. I told him repeatedly that he didn't need to do that as the lawyer always paid for a cab.

Well, Michael does not take no for an answer. He called me around 10:30 pm and told me he was hanging out with his daughter Alexandra, who he had just brought home after dinner. He was insistent on his wish to drive me home. I relented and he arrived at 11:00 pm. I couldn't help but be super happy that he insisted on picking me up. I just did not want him to tire himself out with the long drive from Point Grey to Burnaby and then back to Richmond. Despite taking a driving course in my early adulthood, I never learned to drive. I would often say that it was more danger-ous for a nervous Asian woman to be driving. I would rather walk, take transit or ride a bicycle.

After all, I was going to be seeing him the next day as he had asked me to come and spend the night at his place on Saturday. He said he would drive the long route to my house so that he could spend more time with me. He was happy and very animated. He then shocked me by saying he is wondering who is going to say the L word first. I couldn't believe he brought this up. I was a little cheeky and said to him, which one is that, lust? I was ecstatic that he was hinting that he loves me. He would smile at me and pat my leg

18

and sometimes squeeze it. I was so very happy that this incredible, wonderful man loves me.

We arrived at my place and it was hard to say goodbye to him. I always found it excruciatingly difficult to be apart from him. I will always wonder if I felt this way because I love him, or because he was sick and we never knew how much time we would have. When I first met Michael it was expected that he would only have a matter of a few months left.

CHAPTER THREE
GETTING SERIOUS

February 10, 2007

Michael picked me up from my place in the afternoon. It was a beautiful sunny day and it was a nice drive from Burnaby to Richmond.

We were giddy with happiness, excited and it felt normal. Our relationship had started in the best way possible, with conversation. We never ran out of things to talk to each other about and even when times were tough, and it was hard to talk, we always managed. I really felt that Michael courted me. With emails, it was like love letters going back and forth. I will always treasure those emails as they are precious snippets of our time together.

We went for a walk out by the river in Steveston and took some pictures. I remember the day was cold but it was sunny and beautiful. Although Michael was not a drinker, he knew I liked wine and we stopped so he could buy a bottle of Mouton Cadet to go with dinner.

He cooked me a nice dinner and we had a lovely evening.

For Michael, Love Cynda

Michael and Cynda in Steveston, a suburb of Richmond

February 11, 2007

Michael was a wonderful cook and put great care into the preparation of meals, even when it was a simple meal. He even took care in how he assembled a simple sandwich, for lunch of course. There was order to the placement of each item and the combination of ingredients. I learned from him to always eat good food, otherwise why bother. Also to make the effort to prepare a nice meal and to make sure you did that when you were just cooking for yourself as well. This is something that has stayed with me and I am mindful of making solitary meals special.

It was our first breakfast together, and the first of many that Michael would make for me during our time together. Later on he said that he would make breakfasts for me for as long as he was able and then it would be my turn to make breakfasts for him.

He made Eggs Benedict (one of my favourite breakfasts/ brunches) with lox that he had cured himself from a salmon that he had caught. How Iron Chef and Food Network was that? Once again, he continued to make me feel so cared for and special. It had been a very long time since someone had looked after me with such care.

I did not want to go home but it was time. Our bliss-ful weekend was coming to an end and Michael drove me back to my place.

From: Cynda
To: Michael
Date: Monday, February 12, 2007 2:43 PM
Subject: Yoga Class - More details

Hi Honey!

It is Wednesday evenings from 5:00 to 6:15pm on Cambie at West Georgia.

The address is: 750 Cambie Street, 3rd Floor (turn right when you get out of the elevator and the door is on your left at the end of the hall).

The building door and elevators lock right at 5pm so if you get there and it's shut, just call me on my cell (339-5555) and I'll send someone down to get you.

She has extra yoga mats so you can borrow one there.

Talk to you later.

Cynda

From: Michael
To: Cynda
Date: Monday, February 12, 2007 3:10 PM
Subject: Yoga Class – More details

got it thank you. talk to you this evening. will you call after 10?

XOX Can't believe I miss you!

Michael.

From: Cynda
To: Michael
Date: Tuesday, February 13, 2007 7:42 AM
Subject: Good morning

My dearest Michael:

I thought I would send you this email before I leave home and get involved in another busy and hectic day.

Hope you were able to get some restful sleep last night. I wish I was there to put my arms around you and to hold you. To stroke your cheek and kiss you but I will tomorrow evening.

Since I met you I have had so much extra joy in my life. I didn't think it was possible to be this happy. I feel like a giddy teenager. Maybe that is why I have more zits on my chin right now than I have had in ages.

Going with you to get your golf clubs was special because I got to share in something that made you so happy. Sitting on the sofa listening to music or watching golf or the Elvis movie with you I felt content. I am so happy with you and I can only hope and pray that you will be in my life for many years to come. We deserve the happiness. I have to believe that after years of hardship you are my just reward.

Just keep hanging on to the positive and good thoughts and put any dark ones in a box and put them in storage. Leave the darkness as you don't need it. You can do it as you are strong.

Think often of years to come, walking Alexandra down the aisle, holding her kids, watching your grandchildren walk, seeing Eric become a Dad and watching him teach his son how to fish and golf and you watching and smiling and pointing out to Eric just how great it was when you taught him when he was young. Think of both of them coming to you for advice on potty training and everything else that grandpa would be part of.

Think of sunny and warm days holding my hand and walking along the beach, stopping, taking in the happiness of the day and wondering what outfit I will wear later that night. Think of cold winter days, warming my cold hands and sitting in front of a roaring fire.

You make me complete.

XOXOXOXO

Cynda

Talk to you later honey. Have a great day.

From: Michael
To: Cynda
Date: Tuesday, February 13, 2007 10:06 AM
Subject: Good morning

Those are the nicest words anyone has ever said to me.
I cried.

Michael

CHAPTER FOUR
TEST RESULTS

February 13, 2007

Today Michael had to go to the BC Cancer Agency Clinic for further testing. On his last visit he had an infection and so the x-rays were not conclusive.

He called me that evening or I called him I think, I can't remember. I was panicked and it had been much too long and I hadn't heard from him. The news was not good. The cancer had become aggressive again. It had been stable since October. They would start him on chemotherapy and they wouldn't wait very long before they started either. I remember tears flowing freely and rolling down my face as I talked to him. I never even thought about being scared. All I could think about was that there would be more suffering for him.

It was a very difficult night and all I could think about was that I would see him tomorrow and it couldn't come soon enough.

To this day, I can close my eyes and see me sitting on the floor in my basement as I tried to absorb the enormity of what was to come. This was real life and it was incredibly scary.

From: Michael
To: Cynda
Date: Wednesday, February 14, 2007 9:50 AM
Subject: Happy Valentine's Day

HAPPY VALENTINE'S DAY HONEY.
Just a short note to tell you that everything you do is
appreciated. You have quickly become a very special
person in my life. Every moment with you is absolute
magic. See you after work.
With Warm affection,
Michael xxox

From: Cynda
To: Michael
Date: Wednesday, February 14, 2007 9:58 AM
Subject: RE: Happy Valentine's Day

Happy Valentine's Day Michael:

Your timing is perfect. One of my co-workers just got
roses and another co-worker is lamenting the fact that her
husband won't send her any. Your note is far better and
more meaningful than flowers.

I think you know just how special you are to me. The time
we spend together is time I cherish. I am grateful everyday
that I found you.

See you later.

Cynda XOXO

February 14, 2007

It was our first Valentine's Day together and I hated
to think it, but it could be our only. Our relationship was so new and Michael was just a bit anxious

as to what was expected of him. He talked about the pressure on guys and how he had checked the prices of flowers. He said his friend Rob who also had a girlfriend was looking into flowers. I told him he was off the hook. Flowers would have been nice as I love them but I learned that he wasn't big on buying flowers and was happier to cook me a wonderful meal, take me out or do something special for me. He spoiled me in so many other ways that as much as I love flowers, it was okay that he felt that way. I jokingly would say that Michael would buy me prawns instead of flowers. He did surprise me once by pulling into a parking lot and buying me red tulips. That was probably the one and only time he bought me flowers.

I told him that for Valentine's Day, what I would really like is for him to come to a yoga class with me. He was receptive to that although a bit apprehensive. I wanted him to take a class with Charlotte who is the lovely yogi who introduced me to yoga. I first took classes with her in an empty office space in the building where I worked. Because of Michael's cancer, I didn't want just any yoga teacher. I wanted Charlotte as I knew and trusted her and she was never concerned about making money but cared most about people and using yoga to improve their lives.

We were to meet in the parking lot by the studio. I was most anxious as it was a tough day for Michael health wise as he was struggling with painful muscle spasms. It was tough for him to make the drive to come to meet me.

We arrived at the studio early enough that there was time to let Charlotte know that Michael had cancer. As expected, she was caring, compassionate and guided him through a wonderful class. She also showed me what I could do to help Michael by pressing down on his shoulders, giving him a good stretch and to help bring him some relief. His shoulders tended to be rounded and a bit hunched over from coughing and being in pain.

I was so happy to share my love of the practice with him. I just wanted to help make him feel better in any way possible. Despite the pain he suffered, he always put on a brave face.

After class we went and had a dinner of noodles and soup. Michael always loved soup and it was one of his favourite foods, although Dim Sum and Chinese pastries were high on the favourite scale.

I had decided that I would tell Michael that night that I was in love with him. It may have been a cliché day to do it on, but it was a good a time as any.

I bought a card that captured how I was feeling. On the front of the card it had a poem that started with the words "With You, I am Me..."

Inside the card I wrote:

> *My dearest Michael,*
>
> *You mean everything to me and I will always be here for you, whatever you need.*
>
> *Since I met you I cannot remember ever feeling more cared for and treasured.*
>
> *I can't possibly understand all of what you are going through. I am not so articulate right now either.*

I can promise to hold your hand always. To comfort you, and to be next to you. Words will not always need to be exchanged.

I am strong and will do everything I can to help you to beat this disease. It can be done. You can always lean on me.

I think I am rambling now and am no longer so articulate, but I do have this to say. Sometime during one of those late night calls and probably even before Colin James, I fell head over heels in love with you.

I love you with my entire heart and soul.

Cynda

In relationships many of us have rules. One of my rules was I would never put my heart on the line by being the first one to say "I love you." I never did until Michael. I would like to believe it was because I was so certain and not because he had cancer.

I already knew and maybe I fell in love with him the first moment I laid eyes on him. I often told his mom that I think I fell for Michael during that first telephone conversation. He was a charming and charismatic man and that voice, he had such a beautiful tone to his voice. It was at times so smooth and others so very funny. He made me laugh and laugh a lot. Despite everything he was dealing with he managed to find much joy in life and I admired him for it.

"When I first saw you I fell in love and you smiled because you knew."

English translation of a line in the Italian opera Falstaff with a libretto by Arrigo Boito

From: Cynda
To: Michael
Date: Thursday, February 15, 2007 11:09 AM
Subject: Hi

Hi Michael:

Chinese New Year at my sister's house is on the Sunday, February 25th at 5:00. You mentioned the 24th.

Try to keep up the breathing and relaxing and you are doing well.

Saturday, maybe the casino? Just thinking.

I love you and those magic hands are not too shabby either.

Love
Cynda

XoXoXo

From: Michael
To: Cynda
Date: Thursday, February 15, 2007 3:31 PM
Subject: Hi

I will keep that date on my calendar. I am glad you are enjoying.

Michael

February 2007

Sometime this month we had dinner with his children, Alexandra and Eric at his apartment. I made my family's steamed dumplings which we called tay, tay. His kids were both really nice and I was relieved

after I met them. I had never dated a man with grown
up children.

February 17, 2007

I first met Michael's mom Mae Chu on a Saturday. At
work the Friday before we had had our annual Chinese
New Year's party and I had brought some left over dim
sum to Michael's. Michael wanted to bring it to his
parents and share the dim sum for lunch.

It was a big deal to meet his mom and although she was
a tiny little woman, she was a force to be reckoned
with and could be intimidating.

She was mindful of me and concerned about me from
the start. When Michael left the kitchen to go to
the bathroom, she took that opportunity to bring up
Michael's health. She put it as delicately as she
could and asked me if I knew about Michael's condition. I told her that yes, he told me about his cancer
and that he was terminal and that he told me this even
before we met.

I know that people would of course question why would
I want to get involved with a man who was terminally
ill. To those that knew and loved him I would respond
with, have you not met Michael? He was so smart,
incredibly charming and made you feel so special. I
knew that by getting involved I had everything to
lose, my heart for one. I had a good job, owned my
home, was physically fit and had raised two sons virtually on my own.

From: Michael
To: Cynda
Date: Tuesday, February 20, 2007 07:11 AM
Subject: good morning tuesday

Good Morning Honey!

Boy I'm up early. Began my day at 6:30 or so. I didn't have a very deep sleep even though I took a cough suppressant pill. Didn't get the drowsies. I'll probably have a nap later I guess. Meanwhile I'm hyper to go over to London and get the phone, seeing they wouldn't sell it to me yesterday nite. The fellow over there said they only had 10 units available today for sale.

Anyway you're my first thought today and I fall deeper in love with you each day. Hope you have a great day sweetee pie.

Michael

From: Cynda
To: Michael
Date: Tuesday, February 20, 2007 11:48 AM
Subject: good morning tuesday

Hi Michael:

You are making my toes tingle right now and I am one big puddle at my desk.

I love you so much it is just unbelievable. I did not think this could ever happen. Not in my wildest dreams.

You are my Prince Charming and I am grateful to have you in my life and for you to feel the same way.

Please make sure you take a nap today and eat properly. You need to be strong and healthy to make it and I need you so much.

I am going to the Art Gallery tonite. Will call you when I get home.

Love you!!!!

Cynda

From: Michael
To: Cynda
Date: Wednesday, February 21, 2007 9:09 AM
Subject: morning Wednesday

Hi Honey,
Just off to Vancouver for club fitting. Slept pretty well without any medications.

...

Love ya honey pie.
Have a good day. See you yogi.
Michael

February 22, 2007

Today after work, we went to a dumpling party at my co-worker Vivian's home along with another co-worker Caecilia. Before arriving at their home we went for a short walk along the seawall. It was a beautiful evening and we had this picture taken by a passerby.

While we were at Vivian's home Michael had a cough- ing fit. Someone asked him if he had a cold and he was honest and told them that he had cancer. They could not believe he was this sick as he looked so well.

Caecilia immediately recalled that I was upset at work recently and now she understood this was likely why.

Cynda and Michael, False Creek seawall

The next day I received the following email from my co-worker Vivian:

> *Thanks for coming last night - we really enjoyed ourselves too. It was wonderful to see you so happy and to meet Michael. What a darling! You both have a great attitude and we are keeping the prayer wheel turning for you both. You seem to be really connected. It's amazing isn't it?? And despite all his interesting life experiences, your coming into his life is what is making him so happy now it seems.*
> *And thanks for the pictures! I love the picture of you two - you look so happy and comfortable. Beautiful!*

February 24, 2007

Michael was on Vancouver Island for the day, spending time with his cousin Michelle for a native healing circle. It was a good break for him to get away for a change of scenery. It was at the healing circle that he bought a beautiful native drum. It hung on the wall at his apartment and after he died it hung in my home for a number of years, until I no longer needed it. I have since given it to Mary Anne, the mother of his children.

I met up with my mom at the mall to tell her before the New Year's dinner that Michael had cancer and was terminal. I wanted to let her know in advance and it wasn't an easy thing to share. As my mother, she was of course, very concerned as she did not want me to be hurt.

February 25, 2007

My family loves me so much. Originally our Chinese New Year's dinner was supposed to be at Abby's home but her husband is more traditional Chinese, and didn't agree to Michael coming to dinner as he and I had only been dating for a short time.

My sister Crystal changed the dinner to her home so that Michael could come. I was nervous, this was the first time that my family would all be meeting Michael. Abby commented that she had never seen me so quiet, ever.

It was a really nice dinner and Michael charmed everyone, including my brother-in-law Allan when he found out about Michael's career with A & B Sound and his vast knowledge of audio electronics equipment.

From: Michael
To: Cynda
Date: Monday, February 26, 2007 10:48 AM
Subject: feeling a bit better

*slept to 10 20 am today, still a bit tired. had lots of leg
cramps that made me jump thru the nite. ready for tay tay
now. Have a great day.please. don't worry bout' me.
check your hotmail. hear from you later*
Michael

February 27, 2007

Michael came over and we took my two love birds over
to a friend of his as they needed a home. I had taken
them because someone else couldn't keep them due to an
unforeseen health issue. Michael introduced me to his
friend as a "rescuer". I guess I have always had the
tendency to try to save creatures and people.

From: Cynda
To: Michael
Date: Tuesday, February 27, 2007 11:35 AM
Subject: Re: thank you for the beautiful card

Hi Honey.

*Sounds good. Hope you got a good sleep last night. I saw
that you read the card in the wee hours of the night.*

*I am sure the sunshine today is an energy boost as I feel
more alive. Glad you feel better. One day at a time.*

Going to Pilates in about 20 mins.
Cyndarella
XOXOO

From: Michael
To: Cynda
Date: Tuesday, February 27, 2007 12:12 PM
Subject: Re: thank you for the beautiful card

You're so lovable.
Michael xxxoxxox

February 28, 2007

Since meeting Michael his toughest health issue was dealing with frequent painful body cramps. He would have a coughing fit and be wracked with terrible muscle spasms. He was amazing and took it all in stride. His bravery in the face of such pain was astounding. He also had some heavy nosebleeds where he would wake up with a bloody pillowcase. These were fortunately not often.

We were trying to book a getaway as I had booked March 7th to 9th for us to go somewhere local for a few days.

March 3, 2007

Tonight was dinner at the home of one of Michael's closest friends, Sam and his wife Lana. It was a very small world as I had had contact on occasion with Sam in the course of my position as a legal secretary. I also knew of his wife Lana as she was in a related industry.

I was nervous, as meeting his friends was a big deal. Also I wasn't a golfer and had no interest in golfing. Michael and I had jokingly agreed that I didn't have to golf and he didn't have to run. He happily shared all our connections with his friends and it was a pleasant evening with a group of really nice people.

March 5, 2007

Michael emailed me a copy of one of his favorite songs, *Somewhere Over the Rainbow/What a Wonderful World* by the late Israel Kamakawiwo'ole, a Hawaiian musician.

When we were in Hawaii he bought the CD. After he died, it happened several times that the song would play at an opportune time. It was as if Michael had caused it to happen or at least thinking that brought me comfort.

Kenny Chesney was Michael's favourite musician and his song *Don't Blink* often made me cry. Once it was playing in the car and Michael commented that the song makes me sad doesn't it? The song played at Andrew's college graduation held almost a year after Michael died. It was like Michael was telling me he was there.

CHAPTER FIVE
SUNSHINE COAST

March 7, 2007

Today we headed to Gibsons on the Sunshine Coast for a three day getaway. I had never been there before and was happy to be spending a few days away with Michael.

Cynda and Michael, on the beach in Gibsons on March 8, 2007

Michael made all the arrangements and we stayed at Hopkins Landing Bed & Breakfast. Our first obstacle was climbing up the long flight of stairs to get to the B & B. The exertion was tough on Michael, but he managed.

We spent this time getting to know each other better. The conversation flowed easily and he told me a great deal about his work life as well as family.

We had leisurely romantic dinners and afterwards we had the use of an outdoor hot tub with a view of Howe Sound. We were the only guests and it was nice and private.

Michael needed a daily nap and one time when he was resting, I took the opportunity to go for a run as I always like to run whenever I am travelling. It gives me a chance to look around and it's a great way to see more sights. The roads were quiet and the scenery beautiful.

We went to a golf course and Michael drove the golf cart and had me driving for a bit, me who doesn't even drive. It was a lot of fun and we laughed a lot.

Michael did a lot of driving on this trip, the weather was perfect and the scenery was lovely. We drove to Roberts Creek as well as Sechelt.

March 11, 2007

Entry in Michael's journal: "3 wks after Docetaxel my hair is falling out!"

March 13, 2007

I emailed my girlfriend Margy who lives in Europe to update her with my life.

Here is an excerpt:

> *Much has happened over the past couple of months. I have met a wonderful man and we are in love. I am very*

grateful as he is the man I have waited for all my life and he feels the same way.

I met him through a dating website back in mid January. You can see what he looks like as well at www.plentyoffish.com. Search for a user named Fred Flounder.

...

We have a great deal in common. The first time I spoke to Michael we talked for 2 hours and would have continued to talk longer except by that time it was well into the night. He is a second generation Canadian like me.

We found out many common things. His mom went to Sunday school with my Aunty Elaine. His family lived in Lillooet and my aunt and uncle lived in Lytton which is about 45 mins away.

His family home I can see from Harriet and James's kitchen window. This is where he lived with the mother of his children who still lives there with his kids, a son and a daughter. They are 19 and 22 and both very nice. I cooked dinner for them a couple of weeks ago.

His aunt and uncle owned an IGA and as you know so did my Grandma.

Another time I was talking about Richard, my former boss and then he asked me what his last name was. I did not clue in although I knew his mom's maiden name, that his uncle was a long time friend of my boss's and I dealt with his uncle on many occasions. His dad knows my uncles. I have met his parents prior to that and they are really nice. He has also met all of my family. I have also met many of his close friends.

He is sweet, considerate, thoughtful, a really good cook, kind, generous, smart and the perfect man for me. So that is all the wonderful stuff about Michael.

The sad part is he is fighting lung cancer. I knew this when I met him. He told me everything that first night when we talked. On our first date we went out for a lovely Japanese dinner and then continued to go out. He was concerned about getting involved. He had been stable for 3 months. I thought about not getting involved as my chances of getting hurt could be great but he is such a wonderful man I decided that life is short and you never know what is going to happen. I also felt that the first man I get involved with after this many years needs to be really special and he is. It is all a matter of better to have loved and lost than never to have loved.

We spend as much time together as possible. I spend weekends with him and 2 to 3 days a week. We talk every night and email and sometimes talk a few times during the day.

He was diagnosed about a year ago and it is not operable as it is too far gone so all they can do is keep him stable. He has undergone five chemo treatments last year and then one since we have been together. He has another scheduled for this Wednesday and tests tomorrow.

We hope that all goes well and that we are able to travel somewhere hot together.

I have quit working all overtime since mid-February, just the weekend before we found out that the cancer was back and the markers have doubled.

I try to be really positive and he is too so that makes a big difference. His hair started to fall out yesterday and that is a tough thing to deal with.

I think God sent me into his life for a reason. Because I have overcome such adversity and survived and am so strong. I no longer have any baggage from former relationships which is wonderful. I am wise and self-assured (he says he loves it that I am this way and I never thought I was but realise that I now am confident.) He says I am his best motivator. I told him that he is good for me too. My life was content but I worked too much and did not play enough. Also that since being with him I have such highs of happiness.

He has been coming to yoga with me and I to the driving range with him. I have gone with him golfing. I watched and he played. I even drove the golf cart. He teaches me things and I teach him. There is a mutual respect and we can talk to each other about everything.

So that my friend in a nutshell is what has been happening. It feels really good to spill it all out to you.

I am going to go for a run now as it is one of our few sunny days. I need the stress relief as well.

Say hi to Marc for me.
Love
Cynda

From: Cynda
To: Michael
Date: Wednesday, March 14, 2007 8:24 AM
Subject: Morning Honey

Because I save everything (being the pack rat in recovery that I am) I wanted to send you the text of this email that I sent you a while back.

I hope the treatment goes well today. Thinking about you every moment.

"My dearest Michael:

I thought I would send you this email before I leave home and get involved in another busy and hectic day.

...

You make me complete.

XOXOXOXO

Cynda

Talk to you later honey. Have a great day."

I love you and always will. I know you will fight like hell today for all the many people that love you so much.

Talk to me after the treatment, okay. My cell battery is weak as I forgot to charge it but call me.

From: Michael
To: Cynda
Date: Wednesday, March 14, 2007 09:41 AM
Subject: Re: Morning Honey

Honey pie,

That was so nice to read again. It's so meanigful and keeps everything in perspective. As realized, I had great difficulty sleeping. Slept between 5 to 9 until wakened by phone call from friend Henry. He's invited me for dinner next Monday to listen to his new spkrs [speakers]. Henry was my former business parter of 12 yrs. Had some real moments last nite. Started my letter to my son. Every minute goes by and I love you more and more each second.

Michael.xxxxox

March 14, 2007

Michael started his chemotherapy treatment. He always seemed to tolerate the treatments well. If he ever vomited, I never knew about it. Afterwards he would just be tired and would sleep.

From: Michael
To: Cynda
Date: Thursday, March 15, 2007 10:27 AM
Subject: hi, good morning honey pie

Hi My Honey pie,
I luv u so much. You are my sunshine. Look at all the puddles under your seat.

Anyway had a good deep sleep, although short. Had difficulties getting to sleep, had a nap just after our phone call to about 2. Got up and had a sandwich (steroidal feast) and H2O and tried to sleep again, but it took till about 4am.

Up at 930. Got to go to a fax machine over at Kinkos. and meet Mom and Baree for golf just after noon. So have a good day and if I feel okay after I will phone you either way about this eve.

...

Love you so much you wouldn't believe!!!! Baldy (no his name was Valdy)
Michael
xxxxxxxxxxxxxxxxxxxxxxxxxxxxxxxxxooooooooooooooooooo
ooooooxxxxxxxxxxxxxxxxxxxxxxxhug hug

From: Cynda
To: Michael
Date: Monday, March 19, 2007 8:58 AM
Re: Hi

Hi Honey:

Thanks again for taking me to the bus. I really appreciate it. Thanks for packing me lunch and making me coffee and breakfast and taking such good care of me.

I got here at about 10 to which is perfect and I start work in a couple of minutes.

Miss you already.

And just so you know, each day I am constantly amazed that we found each other and that I grow to love you more and more.

Cynda

XOXOXOXOX

From: Michael
To: Cynda
Date: Monday, March 19, 2007 9:03 AM
Subject: Re: Hi

Hi, Glad u got there safely. Enjoy your lunch from the Master. Lana thanks you for the cookie recipe. Got your

text messg too. Love you have a good day. Hurry home.
We gotta go to T town. [T and T Supermarket] tonite.

Michael xxxxooxxxooxxxooooooxxxx

March 19, 2007

That evening we had dinner at the home of his friend
Henry and his wife.

March 2007

Michael had agreed to housesit for his Aunty Shirley
and Uncle Tim while they were away. They were not
related by blood but very dear friends of his parents
for many years. They lived in a large, beautiful older
house in a nice part of Vancouver and we would be
house sitting for about 10 days. But more than just
house sitting, we would also be looking after their
cat Wispy.

Michael would head over to the house in the morning to
let Wispy outside and play with her. She was a tiny
fluff-ball of fur that you instantly fell for.

I often met him there after work for dinner, and later
we would head back to his place.

Michael was really excited about playing house and it
was like being on a holiday. The downside was no sofa
to sit on to watch TV. There was a spare bedroom in
the basement where we would take naps. We never did
spend the night there as it was more comfortable at
his place.

The first meal he cooked there was most memorable. He
wanted it to be a surprise and it was. He made Pad
Thai, one of my very favorite dishes. Another dinner

was rack of lamb. My thoughts were boy could he cook, and I am gonna get fat. Yikes, gotta run and exercise. We also had one dinner party there and Michael made surf and turf for a few friends.

Michael was in between chemo treatments and was able to go up and down the stairs to the basement although it tired him out. It never ceased to amaze me just how strong a fortitude he had. He had an amazing will and it didn't hurt that he was stubborn as hell.

He told me that the stereo in the living room was one of the very best. We always had it on and played the CDs. A newly discovered favourite was a Rod Stewart one called The Great American Songbook which was full of old classics.

Michael had worked in the home electronics business for some 10 years at A & B Sound. I spent many hours at that store and was there almost weekly. Chances are good our paths crossed.

I loved to dance and I knew it would be far too much exertion for Michael and so it was not an option. One evening while dinner was cooking he surprised me. We were in the living room listening to music when he took my hand and danced with me. He spun me around smoothly and it will always be one of the happiest and most tender moments for me. He said he always thought he would be good at dancing. All through-out our relationship and frequently in the beginning, Michael would say to me "Sweetee it all just comes to us easily".

Shortly before our trip to Cuba we went to Zellers (a department store) at the local mall as Michael wanted to purchase a new watch. He became frustrated with the sales clerk and ended up yelling at her. I was mortified and didn't know how to deal with this. We left the store and in the parking lot I was crying and I told Michael I couldn't be with him if he was going to treat people like this. I said to him that just because he had cancer, he couldn't blame other people because he was dying. It wasn't their fault and no one deserved to be treated like that. I didn't know where this version of me had even come from. I was never ever good at speaking up for myself or taking a stand. This was huge for me. He said he felt terrible and that he wouldn't do this again.

I learned from family that he could have a hot temper and be difficult. I thought he was behaving this way because he was sick and taking a steroid called Dexamethasone. I used to tell him that although he could be difficult, he was still perfect for me. I loved him for who he was, imperfections and all. When I was younger I had a very hot temper and I was still like that in my twenties. It took me a long time to learn to control my temper and not freak out about things I couldn't change and control.

Michael's hot temper may have been why he owned a t-shirt that said "I Need Supervision". Now when I see pictures of him wearing that shirt it makes me smile. He had another t-shirt that said "My anger management class pisses me off!".

A few days before our trip to Cuba we went for lunch at Flamingo Chinese Restaurant, our favourite dim sum restaurant to feast on all our favourites. We both were fond of chicken feet and each had our own, calamari as they did it just right, and seen jook geen, a bean curd wrap filled with chicken and vegetables. He always had to practice how to say this and couldn't ever seem to remember it. He would also make fun of Gun Chow Gnoi Hwa, pan fried beef rice noodle.

March 24, 2007

Less than two weeks before Michael's 53rd birthday, his hair started to fall out. It did not with his previous chemotherapy treatments but with this second round, it was expected. One morning, bits of hair started to fall out and there was a lot on his pillow. It was happening quickly and he would sit and pick at his head constantly. Luckily, I found a hairdresser that was still open that Saturday night and so we went to get his head shaved. The hairdresser was wonderfully compassionate and gave us a business card for his friend who was a cancer survivor.

It was an emotional experience for him to lose his hair as he was proud of his full head of healthy hair. Cancer had taken yet another part of him.

March 25, 2007

I told Michael he was very sexy to me and I liked his shaved head. Our next errand would be to find him some earrings. He wanted to wear a stud in his ears and we went to Claire's (a jewellery and accessory store) where he bought fake diamond studs that attached to his ears with a magnet. He would admire his new look in the mirror and smile. Talk about taking something bad and turning it around.

Later that evening, we celebrated Michael's birthday dinner at a local Chinese restaurant. Michael was also debuting his new look and I will never forget the shocked look on Alexandra's face when she saw his diamond studs. She may have thought her Dad had lost his mind. He was also wearing a few more rings, Michael was definitely changing up his look.

He did consider getting his ears pierced but could not decide.

I told him not to do so as it was better for him to save his body's energy to fight his cancer than to heal an optional piercing.

This was the same night that I first met Mary Anne, Baree (his brother) and Molly (Baree's girlfriend). Sam and Lana, close friends of Michael had also been invited to the birthday celebration. I was nervous and anxious. It was a very nice dinner and everyone was very welcoming.

After dinner we went to his parents' home to take pictures and have dessert.

CHAPTER SIX
MICHAEL'S 53RD BIRTHDAY

March 26, 2007

When the plane landed on the runway Michael started to cry. He said he never expected to see this birthday and he was so grateful that he was still here, and that we were in Cuba. I fell more and more in love with him as he was so brave and candid with me. He bared his heart and soul.

Cuba was everything we could have hoped for and it was simply amazing. Michael had wanted us to travel from almost the beginning. I did not have a passport at the time but as soon as it came through he wasted no time in booking this trip. I think we booked it on a Thursday to leave on the following Monday. The trip was also booked quickly as we wanted to go and return before April 4, 2007, when another round of chemotherapy would be started.

Cynda and Michael with our favourite waiter in Cuba

Our trip was idyllic. We spent days lying on the beach. That was new for me as I had never been on a lay around on the beach vacation. My few hot vacations were spent being busy and sightseeing.

We listened to music on our devices and Michael shared his love of music with me. We went to several live shows in the evenings. We checked out the cigars and on one sunny evening we sat outside with a cigar and a coffee for Michael. He and I shared that cigar and I have to admit it tasted fantastic.

We hired a driver through one of the waiters at the restaurant and spent the day in Havana, a few hours drive from Varadero. Michael sat in the front passenger seat and I behind him. It was one of the few times we did not sit side by side. We went for a lunch of langosta (lobster)at a restaurant suggested by the driver. It was up a flight of stairs which was tough for Michael, but he made it.

Cynda and Michael taking a carriage ride

Although we did a lot of lying on the beach, we also wandered around and did a fair amount of sightseeing. We spent one day on the bus and went all over Varadero and back. On another day we walked to the market in Varadero and did some shopping and explored. We were totally in bliss and experiencing Cuba for the first time together was special. It amazed me that we were so in sync with each other so quickly. Like Michael always said "Everything just comes naturally for us sweetee." He was excited that we had a king sized bed in our room as he teased me about hogging it.

We walked along the beach and sat outside late at night and just watched the sky. It was romantic and wonderful. One evening at dinner we each had a glass of wine, came back to our room, lay down for a bit of a rest, and passed out. Strong stuff.

We laughed a lot and when we were at the market I was looking at some items to buy and he came up behind me and started to caw like a crow. I had told him earlier that I was part crow as I liked things that are shiny and sparkly.

We both really enjoyed the music in Cuba and Michael purchased some CDs.

Michael could talk to anyone and everyone. He was always interested in people and he made an effort to ask them about themselves. We became friendly with those that worked at the restaurants as well as the housekeeping staff at the resort.

We returned to Vancouver from Cuba on April 2, 2007.

April 3, 2007

Michael was given a journal for his 53rd birthday. Here is the journal entry for today:

"Golfed with Sam today - great day! Good news at clinic. Best Happy Day in a long time."

He wrote in it sporadically in April, December and then mostly in January 2008 during our trip to Hawaii.

April 4, 2007

Michael's journal entry:

"3rd session 2nd line Chemo treatment today at 11 am. Hoping for no reaction. Hyped on steroids now. Low sleep."

From: Michael
To: Cynda
Date: Wednesday, April 04, 2007 8:02 AM
Subject: time

Hi Honey,

Easy girl, not to quick and hard today. We just spent over the last 12360 minutes together and it was one of the best times I have spent with anyone. Boy do we get along and live and love each other well. I cannot stop believing it. Yesterday was so positive for me. I feel so good, (perhaps the steroids, Fred just won't go back to sleep) Anyway, honey, have a great day . 2 episodes of 24 and a 4am sleep start and wide awake now may influence I don't golf. R U interested in yoga today? Let me know . Golf might be just a bit much today even though I want.

Love Big Freddy (looking for little cynda to come out and play)

From: Cynda
To: Michael
Date: Wednesday, April 04, 2007 4:57 PM
Subject: Re: time

Hey Big Freddy:

I have tears in my eyes as I read this and like I told you I don't cry easily. At least not in public.

Damn good thing I didn't get around to putting on makeup or I would resemble Alice Cooper, the early years right now.

I feel like my left tit is missing .....

Okay, so the top part is what I wrote before you called me.

...without you next to me.

Like I say, you are a mushball. I am so amazingly content with you. Things just fit. We are so lucky. We can laugh, play and be serious and that is not an easy thing to accomplish.

You know that I am so grateful that your test results were good yesterday. It gives us a burst of renewed hope.

Love u

GP

XOXOXO

Hope you took your vitamins and are going to eat lots of veges.

BTW, I did buy a 6/49 cos you never know. I also joined another pool in the office.

Going to silly store now and will be home by about 7 ish. Call me when Idol is on and we can watch it together.

April 7, 2007

We had dinner at the Macaroni Grill restaurant to celebrate the 90th birthday of Mary Anne's mother.

April 10, 2007

Michael's journal entry:

"Bday massage at Spa Utopia today thanks to Cynda. Loved it."

April 12, 2007

Rainbow, the home care nurse spent about an hour with Michael.

> *From: Michael*
> *To: Cynda*
> *Date: Friday, April 13, 2007 3:52 PM*
> *Subject: one leads to two and so on*

ok, sweetee, remember just one little itsy bitsy teeny weeny drink, dont let it lead into two then three and so on even if it is Friday. it was a short week, remember....think of me slaving over the stove and chopping and peeling potato after potato just for your sole enjoyment . remember the slave.

love your love slave,

Michael...xxxxx0000xx

From: Cynda
To: Michael
Date: Wednesday, April 18, 2007 8:48 AM
RE: Thoughts

Hi Honey:

I wanted to say more to you last night but I couldn't get the words out right.

When I was younger and going to Sunday School we learned some verse in the bible that talked about everything dying and that all things turn to dust. I was annoyed by the whole prospect and just thought then what is the bloody point of it all then if nothing lasts forever. For a while I didn't want any possessions because I felt like it was all worthless.

I learned years later that if things last forever we take it for granted. As it is, we humans often take life for granted. We assume things will go on indefinitely. Maybe it is just a defence mechanism as most people are scared of the unknown. I know I am sometimes and I either block it out or I tell myself it will all be okay. Of course, no one knows for sure but I have to believe and have faith that when we are all so unique and so complicated that there is more to us than just this physical world.

I have tried to always appreciate life and its fragility and how fleeting it can be. I think having worked on motor vehicle accident files for almost 8 years definitely made me think a lot more. I saw how people's lives could be destroyed or turned upside down in a split second. It made me really appreciate everything.

I don't want you to worry so much, especially about things you cannot change. You need to focus on what you can change. I am so sorry you have such rough nights but I know that it is inevitable. How could you not think about everything.

I think it is nothing short of a miracle that we found each other and then found love as well. We are blessed and lucky. I will be okay. One day, hopefully, a long time away from now, I will hurt and I will cry and I will miss you terribly and I will never be the same but isn't that what life is all about. I never thought I could care and love again. Life is all about learning and changing and feeling. You know I never wanted to date just any guy and I didn't. You are almost everything I wanted in a man and then some.

I want to treasure all the time we have because like you have said before every second is special.

I will always love you and one day, you and I will be together. I think we probably already were in another life. We mesh so well. I was probably one of your concubines back in ancient China.

Anyways, I gotta get to work. I love u and I will talk to you later.

Cynda

XOXOXOX

From: Michael
To: Cynda
Date: Wednesday, April 18, 2007 10:37 AM
Subject: thoughts

Hi Honey,

Thank you for your thoughts. I know you are trying to provide comfort. Just being there and around me gives me the comfort and joy I need. I am very aware that this must be hard for you which gives me great concern. I am so worried about missing my sweetee...You are the sweetee Ive waited for all my life for. i hope you know that.

I got up around 10 after a phone call from Erik, an old friend of mine wanting to hear how well I am. I had some difficulty waking up but have calmed down and breathing ok here at the desk. Still don't know if I feel like doing anything physical like golf. Maybe just stay here and rest my weary bones. I hope your day is going well and you're not too tired. I love you and I hope you can call me when you have a chance. Have a good run today . Watch those legs.

Love Michael. Xxxxxxxxxxxxxx0000000000xxxx

April 21, 2007

This was a special night because I would be going to a celebration of love and commitment with the man I love, the man I have waited my entire life for.

The night was made that much more special because I caught the wedding bouquet. Of the many of weddings I had attended, I had never caught the bouquet. Hoped to many times, and then as years went by, it no longer mattered. Well this bouquet came at me like a meteor and landed with a crash right in front of my feet. I was at the back of the group and it was "meant to be". While I was freaking out about the significance, Michael took it all in stride with his comment of "Everything just comes to us naturally honey".

Catching the bouquet after all these years was ironic, as I have finally met the man I have been waiting for all my life, who might not see next year.

I had always dreamed of finding my soul mate but never dreamed that it was actually ever going to happen. This is the stuff of movies and what little girls and women, young and old dream of finding. It is not something that can be bought or forced to happen. It either does or doesn't.

I was twice married and divorced. Michael had also been married and divorced. Until I met Michael, I was adamant that I would never marry or live with a man again. I wasn't willing to risk the heartache, yet with Michael everything just felt right.

Michael and I had had some conversations about marriage recently. Marriage really scares me, I guess because it led to divorce for me and that was a terrible hurt. Both times I wanted the divorce and so maybe I just wasn't meant to be married. I knew that marriage didn't guarantee commitment. With Michael, although we never did marry, we were committed to each other. We had each others' backs and we never doubted the love for each other.

I did end up telling Michael that if he asked me to marry him, I would not say no and I would be happy to be engaged to him indefinitely. In my heart, I was his and he was mine so I did not need to have marriage. I told him I needed to bring up the subject of marriage because maybe he had been hinting and I just didn't get it. But mostly, it is because, one day, when I no longer have him it would mean more to remember him as my fiancé or my husband. He told me that he had wanted to marry me quite early on and he felt this way before Cuba.

It was also extremely important that if we did get married that it didn't have an impact financially on our children. I never wanted anything financially from Michael. It may sound sappy but the reality was that all I ever wanted and needed was his love.

Michael and Cynda at Wedding

April 23, 2007

Today I was meeting up with Michael at Matt's place in the West End. I was going for a haircut after work and then over to Matt's place to watch the Canucks game and also meet Matt's dad and his wife.

I called Michael as I got closer and he watched me from the balcony and was directing me. He was concerned about me crossing the busy street and had sent me an email about traffic. I know that he was anxious about me getting there. He was also anxious about my getting my haircut as he wasn't sure if I was cutting it short or changing it drastically but he didn't dare say anything about what he wanted me to do. We were still very new and I could see the relief on his face that it wasn't drastically changed. We had grilled lamb chops for dinner along with an organic green salad that Michael brought. It was an enjoyable evening of great conversation, hockey and a delicious meal.

April 24, 2007

I went to the BC Cancer Agency Clinic with Michael. I had started going with him to see his oncologist. We had our deepest talks before and after these appointments. All our hopes were pinned on getting good test results. In the last two or so months his tumour markers continued to go down on each visit and it gave us hope.

As I was usually coming from work, I would meet him in the clinic waiting room. I remember looking at everyone who was waiting, and they were of all ethnicities and age ranges. Before his oncology appointments, he would go to the various labs to have x-rays and other tests done first. After the appointments, if needed, we would go to the pharmacy at the clinic to fill his prescriptions.

Michael would often say after the oncologist appointments that (Dr.) Verdana cannot believe I keep coming back, that I am still here. Because he had an appointment scheduled for August 19, I had to call his office to let them know that he had died. Dr. Verdana's nurse called me back and offered her condolences; her kindness helped to console me.

He said he always went to chemo alone which I always thought was terribly sad. His dad would drop him off and then pick him up afterwards. He wouldn't allow me to come with him as he said he didn't want me to have to see. I did go with him a few times after his oncology appointments so he could visit all of those who helped to give him a longer lease on life. It was always very emotional for Michael and it was one of those times when I admired him even more for his bravery.

After his chemo treatments he would always call me. Sometimes he had a bad or allergic reaction and then they would have to stop.

Today's appointment did not bring us happy news, Dr. Verdana told us that the cancer has spread and they have decided to stop further chemotherapy as it is no longer working. Michael is now going to be taking a tumour inhibitor to try to slow down the growth of the cancer. Also he would now be started on Morphine to help him with his breathing and for future pain management.

I am numb.

I try to focus on the happiness at having found each other, as Michael has said many times that I was made for him, that I am the sweetee he has waited for all his life. I am grateful.

April 25, 2007

Michael had been struggling with headaches. He was trying to figure out if it was his pillow, sleeping position or inability to get enough oxygen. He changed pillows and it was a temporary fix. He said it felt like stress headaches. Sometimes with enough rest he was headache free. Other times he felt foggy and called them droner or Morphine headaches.

The mother of a friend of Michael's was a masseuse, and she would come to the apartment and give him massages on occasion. Other times I would and he also saw a chiropractor on a regular basis.

Evenings are busy as we often see some of his friends in conjunction with watching a Canucks game on tv. Michael spends his days resting/napping, some golfing and seeing his parents. Some Wednesdays evenings he goes to his golf club for men's night.

May 5, 2007

I wanted my kids to meet Michael's, and so I arranged for a lunch at a Japanese restaurant. Andrew had returned from college in the United States a short time ago. He would be bringing his then girlfriend with him who I had not yet met. Jeremy had to work and could not join us. Michael's son Eric was coming but Alexandra wasn't able to make it.

> *From: Michael*
> *To: Cynda*
> *Date: Monday, May 7, 2007 2:26 PM*
> *Subject: call if chance*
>
> *Hi, Honey Pie,*
>
> *Got back from GP. Things not bad, headaches still muscular unless cancer has spread. but if tyllenol gets rid of it in half hour or so he thinks its stress. He gave me weak dose and antibis [antibiotics] for travel if i need.*
> *Call me if you have a chance, if not I understand.*
> *Love u too much.*
> *Michael...xxxxpppxxx*

May 12, 2007

Michael and I went to the Vancouver Art Gallery to see the Fred Herzog exhibition. It was our one and only time at the Gallery. We had really nice time and he happily told others how much he enjoyed seeing all the old photos of Vancouver.

I rarely had headaches but was having stress headaches in part due to being so tired and also grinding my teeth in my sleep. I was still running frequently and getting to yoga as much as possible as it helped me to de-stress.

May 13, 2007

Tonight we had a Mother's Day dinner at Kirin Seafood Restaurant with my family. Michael enjoyed bragging to his mom that we went to Kirin.

> *From: Cynda*
> *To: Michael*
> *Date: Thursday, May 17, 2007 6:16 AM*
> *Subject: Re: time*
>
> *Hi Honey:*
>
> *I got up this morning just before the alarm. I looked to your side of the bed and you were not there.*
>
> *Found you in the living room, bare assed, just the way I like you, sleeping on the sofa. It made me feel warm and smile. You looked so calm and restful. I hope you got somewhat of a decent sleep.*
>
> *All the time spent with you is meaningful. I treasure the silent moments, the mundane ones and the deep ones spent talking about life and death. As tough as it is for me*

talking about a life without you, I know that it is a reality that I have accepted and must face. I just hope not too soon as I will never be ready to lose you.

Don't feel bad. How could anyone be ready to give up something as special as we have been lucky enough to find.

It means a lot to me that you are honest and talk to me so much about how you are feeling. Sharing is so important.

I still pray and hope for a miracle. We have already had some. I hope you continue to have the strength to fight like hell. I am not very religious but I do believe in faith. You were sent to me and me to you for a special reason.

I cannot possibly understand totally how much you struggle daily, physically and emotionally but I know you are stronger than you realise and you have so many people who love you. I hope that this love helps to sustain you to continue to fight.

I have never loved anyone the way I love you and I will always be grateful to have this love. I have also never been loved by anyone the way you love me. No regrets ever, so don't worry.

You will never be just a memory as you are part of my heart and soul.

I will always love you. Don't ever forget it. I do believe we will find each other again one day.

Cynda

XOXOXXOXOX

From: Michael
To: Cynda
Date: Thursday, May 17, 2007 9:19 AM
Subject: Emailing: Michael & Cynda – April 21, 2007 012

*Here's pic just to remind you how much I love u. I know
you are swamped, but just take a minute to enjoy. Love u.
Michael xxooxxxxxxoooo*

[The picture was of us from the recent wedding and it was a favourite.]

From: Cynda
To: Michael
Date: Thursday, May 17, 2007 9:23 AM
*Subject: Re: Emailing: Michael & Cynda – April 21,
2007 012*

*I know you do honey. That is the current pic on
my desktop.*

*In the past couple of months there has never been any
doubt that you love me or how much.*

*Luv you
Cynda
xoxox*

From: Michael
To: Cynda
Date: Thursday, May 17, 2007 11:00 AM
*Subject: Re: Emailing: Michael & Cynda – April 21,
2007 012*

I'm cooking for tonite.

From: Cynda
To: Michael
Date: Thursday, May 17, 2007 11:03 AM

Subject: Re: Emailing: Michael & Cynda – April 21, 2007 012

Okay, honey. Do you need me to pick up anything? I plan to go for a longer run and so expect to leave downtown about 5:20 or so and will be home 6 ish.

From: Michael
To: Cynda
Date: Thursday, May 17, 2007 11:20 AM
Subject: Re: Emailing: Michael & Cynda – April 21, 2007 012

No problem, seinorita, I don't think I need anything. Miguel xxxoooxx

From: Michael
To: Cynda
Date: Thursday, May 17, 2007 12:49 PM
Subject: leaving for kemo [chemo]

Honey Pie,
Im leaving for chemo at@ 120 or so up to mom/dads, will probably finish 330-4 barring any complications. see you at home when you get there, have a nice run, love you,
Michael ..xxxxxoooooxxxx

May 17 - 20, 2007

I arrived at Michael's and he was cooking a pasta dinner. It was definitely not his best as the sauce wasn't right and I think the pasta was overcooked which was not like him. We packed up the leftovers and put them in the fridge. He was in a rush and wanted me to eat dinner quickly as we had to go to the mall. He didn't say why we were going, just that we had to go. Michael never cared to go to the mall unless it was for a purpose. He wouldn't say why he wanted to go there, just that we had to get there before it closed. He was quite out of sorts that night.

I can't remember if he said so earlier or once we got to the mall but he said that we were going to get my birthday gift. He suggested a particular store and I said they had nice jewellery but I preferred to get something in either silver or gold.

He suddenly stopped in front of the Ben Moss Jewellers store. We went to look at diamond rings. I didn't take him seriously until he asked for some rings to be brought out and he wanted me to try them on. He chose one with three diamonds in white gold and asked me how I liked it. He commented that because I have small hands we should get a ring that suits my hand size. He bought me that ring. I really did feel like Cinderella that day. He was so excited and happily showed off the ring.

He told me that he had come to the mall earlier and had checked out the rings and he knew he was going to buy me a diamond ring. Now I understood why dinner was kind of a disaster, he was nervous and so very adorable.

For the longest time I wore that ring on my right hand and after he died, I put it on my middle finger on my left hand where it remains today.

The next day was my birthday. I would be turning 46 and Michael, his children and I were heading to Vancouver Island for the long weekend. We would be staying with his cousins Michelle and Grant.

It would have been a nice break except Michael was feeling so sick. He hadn't been feeling well before that and he had just had chemo on Thursday.

We returned to Vancouver on the Sunday. It was a difficult ferry trip for Michael as he was feeling lousy. He didn't eat much lunch, just some soup and french fries (not the best choice, but he was craving it.)

May 21, 2007

Michael was still really suffering badly with headaches and sleeping on and off much of the day. The nausea had also been quite bad. He blamed it on a natural herbal juice from his cousin Michelle that he had consumed on the weekend on Vancouver Island.

May 25, 2007

Last Thursday was chemo number five for Michael and today is day 10. Things are really a struggle now and life is really tough. In some ways it is harder than I expected and not as hard in some. Strange to put it that way. We all know that we are going to die one day but how does one cope on a day-to-day basis with knowing that your time is going to be shorter. Knowing that you have a best before date? How does one not fall into a vast abyss of despair?

May 28, 2007

MSN conversation.

Michael says:

massive headache

Cynda says:

sorry you have one. Try, if you can to shrug your shoulders and to breathe deeper. Lay on the living room floor and listen to some of that healing music.

Michael says:

call me

Cynda says:

okay, in a couple of mins

Michael says:

k

CHAPTER SEVEN
BRAIN TUMOR

May 28, 2007

I talked to Michael and he told me that his CT Scan was scheduled for today at 4:20 pm. He said that I did not need to go, but I needed to be there for him.

The CT Scan was scheduled as Michael had been suffering from painful headaches, vomiting and other symptoms since before the middle of May. He had been really sick during those past two weeks.

I arrived at the BC Cancer Agency Clinic about 4:10 pm and he was not there yet. I went upstairs to check with the desk to see if he had arrived early and no he had not. I worried about him struggling to get upstairs when he was so unsteady that I went back down twice. The second time I saw his dad waiting outside. I got back upstairs and went to find Michael who was filling out a form and having difficulty doing it. He had me check the form. He looked so tired and the pain showed in his face.

Michael was taken into a room where the CT Scan was performed.

Dr. Ly, who we had seen before, came to see us immediately after the CT Scan was done and told us that
he has a growth of 5 cm at the back of his head.
Ironically, the tumor was about the size of a golf ball
and located in his cerebellum which is, as I understand it, the brain stem. The cerebellum is important
for motor control as well as cognitive functions and
regulating other functions.

The doctor tells us that he has a few months or many
months and that it cannot be predicted. Radiation
therapy will hopefully shrink the growth but cannot
remove it. It is common for lung cancer to metastasize
to the brain. The scan confirmed what we had both sus-
pected for some time as he has had a tougher time with
his thought process, talking and memory.

Michael was immediately prescribed a steroid that
evening and it virtually stopped the debilitating
headaches which had caused him so much pain, nausea,
vomiting and dizziness.

We were told that the chemotherapy treatments for his
lungs would have to stop for now, although he is to
continue with tests. The lucky and really lucky thing
is that the brain tumor symptoms did not come up until
he had already gone through five chemotherapy treatments. The doctor might have only let him have five or
six treatments anyway.

Matt showed up unexpectedly for the CT Scan and it
meant a lot. He came so that he could go back home
with Michael and then they could catch the first NHL
game between Ottawa and the Ducks. It gave me the
opportunity to go home and go grocery shopping for
my sons.

Strangely, we are both feeling okay as he is feeling better than he has in weeks because we now at least know what we are dealing with. Even though everything was still uncertain, we at least know why Michael had been so much sicker lately.

May 29, 2007

I had coffee and breakfast with Michael this morning and it was just like the old days. It made my heart soar to see him feeling so much better. I felt good much of the day and then it started to sink it that I may lose him sooner and then I wanted to throw up. My heart ached and I cried. I did find some cheerfulness as I was grateful that he was feeling better. The steroid took away the pain. It made life bearable for Michael for the first time in weeks.

It is like my honey is back in full force as he was emailing and phoning me. He is cheerful and happy. He had a list of groceries for me to pick up. When I got to his place he was fussing and cooking in the kitchen. It was so good and yet poignant to see him like that.

He made some phone calls and it was tough to hear him talk about death and dying and that he has no fear of dying, just of the pain.

He is happily chatting about golf and is animated and cheerful. Before that he was watching the movie Independence Day and making cheeky comments. Bliss to hear him like that and I savour all these moments and I do my utmost to soak it all in. I want to imprint it in my brain so that I never ever forget this day, these moments and these feelings.

I left work a little late, I made a card for Michael and put a copy of the picture of us from the co-worker's wedding. I left it for him to find during the day tomorrow.

> *From: Michael*
> *To: Cynda*
> *Date: Tuesday, May 29, 2007 9:03 AM*
> *Subject: lucky man*
>
> *I'm sure lucky to have the best woman in town.*
> *I'm the luckiest guy ever, see you tonite...*
> *Michael xxx..OOOxxx*

Despite dealing with a terminal cancer diagnosis, brain tumor and a change in treatment, Michael still managed to have an amazing attitude. We still had chores, groceries, housework, laundry and maybe all those things are good as it makes you focus on the mundane normal tasks. He was also planning for the future as I was sending off his application form to order tickets for the Masters Tournament lottery which would take place in April 2008.

June 3, 2007

It was a Sunday evening and I had a fight with Michael and stormed out of the apartment and went to the mall. My timing was bad though the mall was closing. I got there at about 6:30 or even later than that and it was closing at 7:00 pm.

He had borscht in the blender. It splattered all over him and he got mad that I didn't make him change his shirt first before his did this. This I was sure was just his frustration and brain tumor speaking. He was wearing a white polo shirt at the time. I was spitting mad and left before I said something I would later regret.

When I cooled off, I came back and he was all quiet saying that dinner wasn't ready because I disappeared. He was just sitting on the sofa looking like a sad lost little boy. My heart broke when I looked at him. I apologized and told him how hurt I was that he yelled at me. I told him I would never storm out like that again as it was terribly wrong and unfair of me to do that. He had no idea where I went and asked me where I was.

I was so angry when I left, that when I grabbed my purse, I forgot my cell phone was plugged in and charging.

I bought a dress, a small bag of chips and a chocolate bar. Wine would have been on the list too if I had thought of it. I was really pissed off and ate both of them before I returned to the apartment. The dress I bought at the mall, a red chiffon, became one of Michael's favourites.

> *From: Michael*
> *To: Cynda*
> *Date: Tuesday, June 5, 2007 7:49 AM*
> *Subject: I love my sweetee pie every moment of every day*
>
> *Don;t you ever worry Sweetee, I may not show it all the time, but I love you every minute of every day.*
> *Love BF.*

From: Cynda
To: Michael
Date: Tuesday, June 5, 2007 8:37 AM
Subject: RE: I love my sweetee pie every moment of
every day

Morning Honey:

Although I do know you love me very much, I never get
tired of hearing you tell me. All these emails that you send
to me are love letters and I treasure them. I look forward to
them too.
They are heartfelt and meaningful. Our late night talks are
also very important to me. That is why sometimes I don't
want to go to sleep.

Have a good day and don't overdo it. See you later.

I think of you all the time.

Love Sweetee Pie
XOXO

June 5, 2007

I worked through lunch so that I could leave right at
3:00 and meet Michael at the BC Cancer Agency Clinic
for his every three week visit with his oncologist.

I arrived early, around 3:30 pm and met up with him.
He was happy and was sitting outside the BC Cancer
Agency Clinic on a cement ledge. He was wearing
shorts, his dark blue pullover fleece and baseball cap.
He had gone for blood tests and x-rays earlier. He
happily recanted what he had eaten that day, a doong
(sticky rice wrapped in a dried lotus leaf), udon,
two types of dumplings, a bacon and tomato sandwich,

and some cereal. We laughed. The steroids made his hunger uncontrollable.

We went inside about 3:40 pm and only waited for a very short time before he was called. He would be seeing Dr. Chun as we knew that Dr. Verdana would not be there today.

We had not met with Dr. Michie Chun previously and she was most pleasant. She explained that doctors special- ize in certain types of cancer and that she has been with the clinic for about nine months. She added that she had already worked for a year in the area of lung cancer in another city.

He recanted his medical history for her. He told her what he hoped to be able to do as far as travel over the next two months. He said he would like to fly fish and said that he could work around their dates but just needed to know.

She explained that the current chemo of which Michael had had five treatments could not be given at the same time as the radiation as it would be detrimental to the treatment of the brain tumor which they feel is more important. She explained how the radiation would be given, that it would be broader and not pinpoint as that type of radiation treatment could not be per- formed more than once. The radiation treatments would be a course of 5, 10 or 15 times and that would be decided by Dr. Medfield who Michael is now scheduled to see on Thursday. Michael voiced his intense dislike of Dr. Medfield and his lack of compassion for human beings. Dr. Chun concurred that he is a man of little words but is very good at what he does. Michael then said it was more important that Dr. Medfield was a good doctor than how he felt about him.

The course of chemo of which he had five treatments, would now cease. He would then have the radiation and then after that, it could be a course of chemo in the form of pills. It had always been our understanding that pills meant end of the road as far as treatment went. She said it was not necessarily so and it would really depend on how his body took to treatment. She added that she has a patient that has been on this type of drug for two years now. That information helped to put things in perspective. She did add that after that clinical trials would be the only type of treatment then available and it would be another type of intravenous chemotherapy.

Michael would be seeing Dr. Verdana again probably mid-July.

Today's test results are all good. The x-rays showed that the tumour has either not changed or shrunk but blood tests are not yet back and that is the best indicator of how he is doing. The tumor marker number is not yet back from the lab and the doctor expects to have it tomorrow and will call Michael with the number.

Last time, after tests on May 15th, it was 240 and earlier this year in February it was 590. A great improvement. What caused this change? Happiness, you would like to believe does make a difference.

After the appointment was over, we were picked up by Michael's dad and driven back to their home where Michael retrieved his car and we went back to his place for dinner. He wanted me to do nothing and to just relax.

He had picked up some wakame seaweed salad at a little place close to the hospital. He cooked up a stir fry of broccoli, mushrooms and squid; bacon and tomato fried rice; and we had leftover tofu and roast pork from last night. I think someone has his appetite back and then some.

It was a good thing when he went to his niece's grad that evening, as I got to go for a 52 minute run. Running is my ultimate stress relief and I happily ran in the neighborhood.

June 6, 2007

The home nurse came to see Michael today.

We are planning more travelling, either to his family's lake in the Cariboo or somewhere hot. He nearly booked a trip to the Dominican Republic as the price was right. I didn't want to go yet, at least not until the tumor was dealt with. I didn't want to compromise his health. He wanted to go very badly as the price was right, he adored the Dominican and we were led to believe by the radiologist that another week or two without treatment would not make a difference. Luckily he was unable to book the trip that Thursday night as the next day he heard from the hospital.

> *From: Michael*
> *To: Cynda*
> *Date: Thursday, June 7, 2007 12:24 PM*
> *Subject: tumor marker dwn to 200*

June 7, 2007

We saw the radiation oncologist Dr. Medfield to find out what the course of radiation treatment will be.

He shocked us when he said he would like a consultation with a neurologist and would schedule an MRI within the week. He told us that he felt the tumour could best be treated by being removed. We never expected that surgery was even a possibility and this was miraculous news.

The next day, Friday, Michael called me at work to tell me that two neurologists had seen his x-ray and decided that he needed to be operated on or he would likely only have a month to live. The brain tumor surgery would be scheduled for Tuesday, June 12th. The surgery date was subsequently rescheduled by the doctor for Thursday, June 14th.

Michael was apprehensive about the surgery and commented that he could end up being a bok-choy (a Chinese "vegetable"). His family, especially his mother and I said to him that he had to have the surgery as he needs it.

The likelihood of death from the surgery was 1% and the chances of bleeding or other complications were 5 to 6% so that was also minimal. The neurosurgeon performing the surgery had 23 years experience and worked out of the BC Cancer Agency Clinic so that was reassuring. I know we were even more impressed when we met Dr. Kow and he was impeccably dressed, articulate and personable. If I was going to have brain surgery, this is the guy I would want doing it.

June 9, 2007

I took Michael out for a dim sum lunch at Flamingo
Chinese Restaurant. Afterwards we picked up some
frozen dim sum for home and dropped off a fishing rod
belonging to his friend Kevin to be fixed. Kevin lives
in Montreal and the rod has been in Michael's closet
for months. After we dropped by to have a short visit
with his parents and then headed home.

He cooked a delicious dinner that he learned how to
make from watching Jamie Oliver on the Food channel,
new potatoes, tomatoes and chicken thighs with olive
oil and fresh oregano. We also had curried carrots,
broccoli, cauliflower, onion and mushrooms and then
donuts for dessert. I have gained weight since being
with Michael and as much as it sometimes bugs me,
how can I deprive him of what he enjoys. Because his
time is limited I don't exercise as much and I had
not yet been to the Grouse Grind. (The Grouse Grind
is a vertical 2.9 kilometre trail on the face of
Grouse Mountain. Grouse Mountain is located in North
Vancouver about 25 minutes from downtown Vancouver and
is popular for hiking, snowshoeing, snowboarding and
skiing.) I loved doing the Grind, it was a bucket list
item for me as I used to be really overweight and terribly out of shape. I still run and take Pilates but
it definitely has been a struggle as there not as
much time to participate in these activities. I come
to his place right after work and so I don't run much.
Life for him will be so much shorter, I don't want to
lose any moments.

June 10, 2007

Sunday morning and I am in Michael's office catching up on my emails. He is in the kitchen cooking a breakfast of very lean bacon (his favourite), eggs and new potatoes.

That evening we had a family dinner, my sons along with Michael's family for hot pot out in Richmond. This was the first time that my sons will meet his whole family. Andrew and Jeremy had only met his son Eric before.

Michael had a habit of using toothpicks, all the time, and I mean all the time. I would have to carry some in my purse, the individually wrapped cellophane or paper ones, so he could get a fresh toothpick whenever he wanted one. At dinner he was playing with a toothpick and I told him a few times to stop playing with it. He ignored me and continued to play with the toothpick. I think I had just said something to him again when his front tooth popped out of his mouth. Now he looked pretty damn funny and he howled with laughter and so did everyone else.

Sundays were family dinner night. Sometimes Andrew and Jeremy would come out and it would be a large group. Other times it would just be Michael's children. As we crammed so much into our weekends sometimes the dinners were tiring events, but I looked forward to them along with Michael. When you are terminally ill there is a sense of urgency as your time is limited.

From: Michael
To: Cynda
Date: Monday, June 11, 2007 9:43 AM
Subject: Just waiting now...and packing soon

Sam called already. Make sure things are okay. Anyway it sure is nice. Changed all the bedding so we have a fresh made bed sweetee. I'm going to turn off the electronics and computer. You can come here anything you know. I'll talk to you later. You can mail me and remind me what I might have to bring to hospital.
Love BF

From: Michael
To: Cynda
Date: Monday, June 11, 2007 12:20 PM
Subject: domestic bliss

Hi Sweetee,

Your laundry is hangin, drying nicely. All is done for you. Domestic burdens all done by slave.
Love you sweetee.

From: Michael
To: Cynda
Date: Tuesday, June 12, 2007 7:49 AM
Subject: don't buy soup

Hi Honey Pie,

Hope you made it to work in a timely manner and got a seat to have you snooze on the way. ... By the way, don't buy the lobster bisque today as I'm making chicken soup for our Ramen tonite okay. I'll try to get some ingredients on the way home. Am going golfing with Baree and Jeff the mess at 11:30 today down at ... it probably takes 4

½ to 5 hrs to pay there, so won't be done till 4:30 or so.
Still lots of time and its a beatiful day. I'm going to rest
for a couple of hours first though. Look for you on email
real soon.

Love
Michael xxxxooooxx

Michael had been golfing with Jeff for a number of years, and coincidentally my father had known him for years through work.

June 13, 2007

Michael was now at Lions Gate Hospital for the brain surgery. He was golfing earlier that day when he received a call that he was to go to Lions Gate Hospital and check in. Surgery could not come soon enough as the medications were no longer helping.

That evening I had many lengthy conversations with Mae while we were sitting around at the hospital.

She queried me about my getting involved with Michael considering the circumstances. She said she wondered why I "latched on to him". I responded that I have met many people over the years and there hasn't been a man that interested me so much. Also I answered "and get my heart broken".

She added that she feels that he has found something in me that he has been looking for, for a long time.

She also asked how my parents felt about Michael. I said my Mom doesn't say much and is coolish and my Dad, after surviving two strokes is pretty happy go lucky. I told her all my siblings like him and most importantly my sister Abby who I am closest to approves of Michael. I also told her that Abby is really glad that I went for a Chinese guy.

She said that yes it is easier to date someone Chinese as there is less explaining and more cultural things in common. I added that I agree and that it is one less hurdle to deal with. She says that with me he is more patient, takes his time more with things and is calmer.

I told her that we never run out of things to talk about. She agreed that that is the most important aspect of a relationship.

Today I talked to the wife of a good friend of Michael's. I commented that I am not big on togetherness all the time and that he wants the togetherness even more than me and I don't know if it is because of the circumstances. I do know that being with Michael is just so good and I am so happy. She said it is because he is in love. I added that I have no regrets that I got involved with Michael.

June 14, 2007

Michael's surgery was a success. Radiation therapy will follow after the surgical wounds heal. The incision was quite long and was straight down the middle of his head. It started about 1/3 from the top of his head and went all the way down to about three inches past the base of his neck. We took several photographs of the various stages of his healing incision.

I was waiting for him as he came out of recovery and the nurse was looking at me and he asked who is that and she replied that it was me. He said "I'm fine,

I'm fine" in a gruff tone. I knew then that he was really okay.

He was kept in recovery about half an hour longer to ensure that his breathing was okay.

Back in his room he wouldn't stop talking all afternoon, he was totally himself again and it was wonderful. He dozed on and off for brief periods. He ate soup and pears for dinner and then had some cantaloupe that I brought and then more soup. The nurse even went to check the stats for the U.S. Open as he had no TV in his room.

Baree came to visit in the afternoon and they discussed golf and fishing. His appetite is good and other than feeling like he has a donut at the back of his head he was doing well.

I was so relieved and happy that the surgery went well and then it hit me...the brain tumor is gone but the cancer is still there. The surgery had bought us more time, not just a month, but a whole precious year and almost two months more.

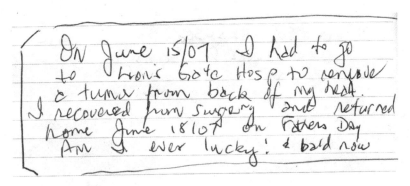

Michael June 18, 2007 Journal Entry

For Michael, Love Cynda

June 27, 2007

Today Michael started to lose his appetite. He had an upset stomach but still managed to eat lunch that day.

That evening we were going out for dinner at the Richmond Boathouse with three golfing couples.

One of the couples came to pick us up and the wife was in a mood that evening, so it was a very tense car ride to the restaurant. This really upset Michael and he had little appetite. He took an antacid in hopes of feeling better. He was only able to eat a small green salad and had a taste of someone's fish and chips. He kept falling asleep at dinner and I know that it was very tough for everyone to see him that way.

June 29, 2007

Michael showing off his new John Fluevog shoes

One weekend we spent a day in downtown Vancouver which was unusual for us. Michael hated downtown and I worked there, so I avoided being there on the weekend. We ate at Wings on Granville Street and we also checked out a lot of stores including John Fluevog Shoes. As we were walking past the store Michael spotted some shoes in the window and stopped dead in his tracks. He spotted a pair of crazy cool shoes and had to have them. Eric always giggled whenever Michael wore those shoes and they made him so happy. Michael had always been a sharp dresser.

June 30, 2007

It was a sunny but windy day and Michael and I had a picnic with Alexandra and spent time at Locarno Beach.

July, 2007

Radiation therapy started the first week of July, just two weeks after the brain tumor surgery.

> *From: Michael*
> *To: Cynda*
> *Date: Friday, July 6, 2007 9:14 AM*
> *Subject: Im up*
>
> *Hi Honey,*
>
> *Ok I'm up now. Gonna eat something/ Don't feel too bad except very sore and stiff like i just had surg [power surge] on that spot. Either I didn't have enough steroid or took wrong item or swelling just plain increased phenomenially. I think the later as radiation is cumuliative. Well starting to feel better, just need to monitor blood etc. Miss you already, better come home right away so we can get a quick start on our wkend.*
> *give me a call or email if you can . leaving at about 1015 or so. Gotta stop at dads*

Love u,
Michael xxxx0ooooxooxx

From: Cynda
To: Michael
Date: Friday, July 6, 2007 9:11 AM
Subject: Re: Happy Friday

Honey:

Hope you continue to feel better after taking the steroid.

I did see a glimmer of the guy I love amongst your pain. I would never be mad at you waking me up when you are suffering, don't you know that?

Anyways, busy day ahead.

Talk to u later. Enjoy your massage. You need it.

Love u
Cynda

XOXO

From: Michael
To: Cynda
Date: Friday, July 6, 2007 9:47 AM
Subject: Re: Happy Friday

You always seem to make it sound like work is so, so, important. and I know youre upset when I interupt your rest so you can function well at work. I get so upset myself, when I know this is happening to you.because I really know it is so important to you to perf0rm at your best at all times. I wouldn't want it any other way myself. Maybe I'm getting to a point where I might be a little more difficult to be with now and you might consider off setting time at your home. I might be getting a little sicker maybe which might get harder for you. I gotta go now to get a plunger to fix the toilet cause I'm your handyman.

Bye for now,

Love BF

From: Cynda
To: Michael
Date: Friday, July 6, 2007 10:08 AM
Subject: Re: Happy Friday

Hi Honey:

Work is important as I am the sole wage earner and I support two kids. I try hard not to screw up. Having to supervise and be available to answer many queries of the junior secretary and associate is sometimes stressful. I also have to deal with other associates too. There are days when I feel very much like the information kiosk at the mall. Work has definitely been harder since last fall...

BTW, since I met you I often and generally don't give a damn about work but force myself to because I have to be responsible.

When you say that I should have remembered to remind you about your shoes, I feel bad. You might be joking but I do take it to heart.

Like I said last night because you were upset about the toilet and I did not know you were suffering it made my response different.

If you can't see how important you are to me, I don't know what else to do. I want to be there for you and I don't intend to leave unless you want me to. Sometimes I get a little testy too when you told me twice yesterday to move over and I already was. You didn't feel good and I didn't know you were in so much pain.

I have been with you when you were much sicker and I intend to always be there for you.

Love u
Cynda

Talk to me more tonite, okay?

From: Michael
To: Cynda
Date: Wednesday, July 11, 2007 11:42 AM
Subject: disc

Sweetee,

If its possible, can you go up to "Virgin" and get me the disc I finally found. Its rare and only there. A guy Michael is holding for me in "Classical Section"
Its called the Hilary Hahn/Nathalie Zhu – Mozart Violin Sonatas. (Duet we heard)
Its about 23 dollars, I would appreciate if you can get up the store. Thanks honey pie
Love u. Can you let me know
Michael xxxxoo

We spent many an afternoon in Michael's living room listening to music.

We both liked to barbeque and enjoyed many meals sitting on his balcony this summer. Michael had planted annuals in some hanging baskets which made it even nicer to be out there. Patio lights added ambience after dark.

From: Michael
To: Cynda
Date: Thursday, July 12, 2007 7:43 AM
Subject: driving

left at 745 for golf course. going to play 9 holes. to change things up. call cell if u wish. Hope youre not too tired today, sorry. for that. Have a nice exercise day. Watch the carb.
Love BF

From: Cynda
To: Michael
Date: Monday, July 16, 2007 8:41 AM
Subject: I Love You

Hi Honey:

In my stupor last night I know you told me several times that you love me. I love you lots too.
I love my diamond ring because it is from you and also because of what it represents. I think of you everytime I glance at it. No need to worry about me. I am okay.

You are getting better every day. Don't forget that. Just keep focusing and doing what you are doing. Don't let losing the St. Michael's bug you because I think that threw you off yesterday.

Do some stretching today and I can help you tonite as well.

...

Love u and talk to u later
Cynda

For Michael, Love Cynda

July 19, 2007

We had dinner with Michael's family to celebrate his parent's 56th wedding anniversary. Pictures taken that night show Michael looking happy, smiling and feeling so much better.

July 22, 2007

We had my work summer picnic and I brought Michael. He was charming and chatted up everyone. It meant a lot for me to introduce him to the people I worked with. It was tiring for him though, and he fell asleep in a chair.

August 2, 2007

We were going to Kelly Lake, located close to Brooke Valley, BC to spend the BC Day weekend with Michael's son Eric, Eric's best friend Vince and my sons, Andrew and Jeremy. Michael's Aunty Lola and Uncle Clifford lived there.

It was a very special time as the lake was a favourite place of Michael's. It meant a great deal to me that he wanted to bring me there. After he died, Eric and other family members returned to the lake to spread some of his ashes.

Kelly Lake

Even though he hadn't been feeling well, going to the lake gave Michael a boost of energy as he was so happy to be there. Before the trip he baked some special muffins which he and I ate at the lake. He also baked a second batch that did not contain any special ingredients which he shared with Aunty Lola and others. Aunty Lola could not say enough about how much she liked the muffins. I think I threatened him with broken limbs if he mixed up the muffins and shared the wrong ones with Aunty Lola.

We stayed at the Kelly Lake Fishing Camp which Aunty Lola and Uncle Clifford used to operate. The fishing camp had not been operating for a number of years and sat idle for the most part. We had the lake to ourselves and I will likely never experience anything more beautiful in British Columbia. It was just us in the lake fishing. I was in one boat with Michael, and the boys went out together in another boat.

There were a few tense moments though, as poor Andrew had the bad luck of breaking one of the fishing rods. I had never gone fishing before but had always wanted to try fishing and was excited at the prospect.

We met some of the other family members, Aunty Lola and Uncle Clifford's daughter and her son. We ate what we caught and we caught a lot of Rainbow trout which we ate for breakfast, lunch and dinner. This may have been the most special of all the trips that I took with Michael as the lake meant so much to him.

Cynda and Michael on August 4, 2007

We tried to focus on quality and not quantity. This was something Michael would often say to me as we had no say as to how long he would live.

CHAPTER EIGHT
CANCER DRUG - TARCEVA

August 10, 2007

Things are getting tougher and life has been difficult. After returning to Vancouver from the lake, Michael started taking the drug Tarceva. Side effects are numerous and comprise of a rash that is like acne, appetite loss, bloating, tiredness, low and mid back pain. Tarceva is a drug specific to treatment of non-small cell lung cancer. It interferes with the growth of cancer cells and slows their spread.

I put moisturizer on Michael frequently as Tarceva dried his skin out so badly it was like his skin was burned. The loss of appetite was difficult for him as he enjoyed cooking and eating.

There were two really rough nights that first week with a calm day in between and then the weekend. I went to work on the Saturday and was exhausted. It was a shitty Friday at work to boot and so that did not help.

The week flew by quickly. I managed to get to exercise for the first three days of the week which helped, but still no running or Grouse Grinding. I was on hormone replacement therapy (I had a hysterectomy in 2002 as pre-cancerous cells were found in my uterus) and was trying to wean myself off. Exercise helped with eliminating side effects. I would stay at this level for probably a month and then see if I can cope without anything. I wanted to be calm and not overly emotional so I did not want to go without the HRT (hormone replacement therapy).

Things are different now. I reminisce fondly of the days when the romance was new and life was happy. I feel so sad some days as it is really tough at times. This past week was one of the hardest with Michael having to deal with so many side effects and not feeling well. You then wonder if it is worth taking the medications. Last Thursday he talked about quitting the drug. I immediately panicked and couldn't get the thought of losing him out of my head. I just kept visualising losing him and crying. After basically watching him sleep and suffer over the past two days I decided that if the drug extends his life but he has no quality, I would rather he be off of it. I did ask him not to stop the drug without talking to the doctors first. Yesterday was particularly bad as he spent almost the entire day sleeping. Sunday is much better and he is more alert.

All I can say is that I still don't have any regrets for getting involved with Michael. I do of course wish for a miracle, how could I not? I am angry at times as this is the man I have waited my whole life for. It is not fair that when I finally found him, it will only be to lose him. It really sucks. I think I am hormonal as well, my emotions are all over the place. I feel like I have lost my kids as our relationship is strained. For so long my only role has been mom.

From: Cynda
To: Margy
Date: Sunday, August 12, 2007 8:08 PM
Subject: RE: news

Hi Margy:

Finally, there is a moment to write to you. Since I last wrote to you Michael has had the brain tumor surgery in mid June. It all went well and it has now been nearly 2 months since the surgery. His scar has faded and there is still a bit of swelling but most of it is gone. He had an infection in his chest which has since cleared up and since early last week he has been working to get his energy up.

We did finally get to go away to his family's lake on the BC Day weekend and that was not only spectacular but very emotional. He never thought that he would get to see the family lake again. On Thursday, August 2nd, Michael and I went to my house and picked up a semi comatose Andrew and Jeremy. Jeremy would get to spend the entire time with us (August 2 to August 5) whereas Andrew was only able to come up for the one day as he had to return to Vancouver by Greyhound on the Friday. He had to work on Saturday at Horizons as there was a big wedding there. You would be proud of me. I fished, and I caught fish. 7 of them. Rainbow trout that was so good. Jeremy caught his first fish but then was not particularly interested in venturing out in the boat again. He actually caught about 5 in total but wasn't able to bring them in. Andrew caught 3 fish.

Michael and I went fishing in the morning, sometimes after lunch and sometimes in the early evening. It was great. Intimate and relaxing. We did get caught in a storm. First I lost my hat, then he his. Unfortunately his sunglasses sank to the bottom of the lake. We managed to get our hats back, were soaked in the rain and came back a little bit stressed but happy nevertheless. Michael and I stayed in a cabin by ourselves and Michael's son Eric and his best friend Vince stayed in another cabin with Jeremy and Andrew. His daughter wasn't able to get enough time off of work and so did not make the trip as she would have had to drive by herself. Michael drove the entire way and did fine. I think he was on such a high at being able to make the trip. His Aunt and Uncle were great. Such sweethearts. Married for 53 years. Michael's parents have been married for 56 years.

I did the yogathon with Michael's brother's girlfriend Molly. After the Yogathon I received very sad and tragic news. My sister's brother-in-law died while trying to save his son from drowning. They had been back east on a family trip. [I was so very sad for several weeks. I kept thinking about his wife and children. His death made me question life and the unfairness of how this could happen to such a good person.]

...

Afterwards, I narrowly missed meeting my own demise by crossing Fraser Street to catch the bus to go back to the office. I tell you, it only takes a split second. A car was stopped for me to cross and the car in the next lane sped through the intersection. If I wasn't paying attention which could easily have happened on this particular day, I would have been a casualty.

It really made me think about life and death even more. We are all just little bugs that could be snuffed out in a split second. Never take things for granted. You really don't know how long you have. I guess I get morbid sometimes as I think about a life without Michael and I just want to die. I also have had a niggling feeling for the past few months that I would die before he does. Maybe it is simply because I don't know how I would face a world without him in it. He really is the love of my life. He is not perfect. He can be a pain in the ass. He is bossy, anal and particular. But he is hilariously funny, goofy, sweet, sensitive and caring.

When we got to his family's lake and he introduced me to his aunt as "his girl" it made me feel so warm inside. Sometimes I get bitter that I won't have a lifetime with him but then who is to say what a lifetime really comprises of. Is it time in minutes or is it quality of the time.

I worked yesterday which he was not too happy with me about but things have been anything from hectic to insanely busy of late. Friday night he and I had a great Japanese dinner at a place called Kiyo which is our favourite high end restaurant in Richmond. Last night it was dinner with is son Eric and then Eric leaves for Cancun tonight with 3 friends. We watched Dreamgirls after dinner, just Michael and I. He had not seen it but I had at the theatre and I wanted to buy the movie.

Right now we have had breakfast about 1 hour ago. I made some whole wheat pancakes, sausages and cantaloupe and dark brewed coffee. Michael is watching/ snoozing to the Food Network. We only got up around 9 because he was really hungry.

We are going out soon to go to buy him some sort of hat as his head gets cold.

Anyways I digress. I wanted to tell you that on July 31st we had another BC Cancer Agency Clinic appointment and he was told no more Chemo as it would no longer be effective but that he would be started on a course of pills. This was a possibility late in March and he wasn't too happy about it at that time as he was told then that he would probably live only to mid July. Well, so much for that as he is still around and I hope to have him for Christmas.

Anyways they have now put him on the meds. He was really reluctant to go on them because if they don't work, that is it. I think the only option would then be trial meds which he is really against. Anyways it has been a week now. This drug is only two years old and would slow the growth of the tumor. It is called Tarceva and one of the side effects is a body rash. They want him to have that sort of reaction because then it means that the drug is working. Happily, yesterday he broke out all over in a rash. He was super itchy the night before. I am grateful for each day although there have been many a difficult night as he has some bad cramping in his legs and chest. Some times his cough is so heavy he had a hard time catching his breath. But he laughs and keeps soldering on.

Dinner tonight is with friends of his. I really hope by some miracle that you get to meet him.

I will send to you some pictures of our trip to the Lake in a separate email. It is 90 mins outside of Kamloops. ... It was like heaven on earth. I know it meant so much to him to be there. I told him at the Lake that this trip was the most important one to me because he loves the place so much.

Take care.

BTW, really like and enjoyed the Hamburg pics. I assume that is your aunt in the pics that you are close to.

Say hi to Marc.

Love u
Cynda

August 22, 2007

Although he was not feeling well, Michael managed to go golfing with friends, one of whom was in town from Hawaii.

> *From: Michael*
> *To: Cynda*
> *Date: Thursday, August 23, 2007 9:17 AM*
> *Subject: breakfast*
>
> *so much for eating. got up here at nine. had pills .*
> *reheated chow mein , had one bite and spit it out , down*
> *the sink , yuck. nothing tastes good.*
>
> *Did you get there on time. I havent heard from you. I think*
> *I'll just go back to sleep and have the tarceva in a couple*
> *see you after, love u*
> *Michael*

Although Michael needs a great deal of rest and sleep we did manage to see Christopher Cross perform at the PNE (Pacific National Exhibition) with Matt. We also had dinner with Alexandra another night.

September 1, 2007

We left for the Dominican Republic. It was my first time and Michael's second. It was a very different vacation than our earlier one to Cuba. We went during the first week of September to take advantage of the Labour Day holiday.

We had a six hour layover in Montreal and arrived around 12:40 am. This gave us the opportunity to meet up with Kevin, a friend of Michael's who lived there. Michael met Kevin when he was making a sad attempt at fishing along the Vedder River in Chilliwack, British Columbia. Michael took him under his wing and taught him how to fish. They became fast friends and fishing buddies. This was just the kind of man Michael was.

Kevin's mother kindly made us a meal of northern pike and walleye. It was a really nice visit and it made Michael very happy. Kevin drove us around parts of Montreal for a bit of a tour although it was in the early hours of the morning. We had to be back at the airport to catch our flight to the Dominican which was leaving at 6:45 am.

On arrival to the resort, we found out that our room was on the third floor, and as there were no elevators, there was no way Michael would be able to climb the stairs. I got our room changed to one on the main floor.

Michael was still struggling with having an appetite. He was not hungry, did not enjoy his food and as a result he was losing weight and muscle mass. His once strong legs had turned into frail, skinny stick legs. Much of the trip was lying on the beach and enjoying the warmth of the sun. Michael did enjoy the pool though and that was good to see. I have a wonderful picture of him scowling at me while standing in the pool. His mom let out a hearty laugh when she saw this familiar expression.

We did get his and her beach massages though and that was a treat. We never left the resort as Michael had done so on his first trip to the Dominican and it would have taken too much energy in any case. I was constantly worried about him.

We returned to Vancouver on September 9th.

> *From: Michael*
> *To: Cynda*
> *Date: Wednesday, September 12, 2007 3:23 PM*
> *Subject: flet survival*
>
> *flet very little chance of survival. Cant take.honey gone too long.*

Despite everything Michael was still incredibly positive and funny. It was a tough juggle as he had nothing but time on his hands, whereas I worked full-time at a busy job, struggled to find time to exercise, spend time with my sons and rarely saw my friends as there just wasn't enough time.

While I was with Michael I gained confidence and I was no longer as intimidated by attempting to cook or bake something new. For Michael, I learned to make chicken pot pie from scratch as well as soft pretzels. I surprised myself at how capable I really was.

> *From: Michael*
> *To: Cynda*
> *Date: Friday, September 21, 2007 12:53 PM*
> *Subject: its been hrs*
>
> *Honey, Its been literally hrs since I've heard from you. I know you got a lot to do as your last messg stated. U must be real busy eh. I went all the way out to Que Pasa at the end of No. 5 road and got tortillas, salsa and juarita pop. Then I went to Save On and had a run in with a clerk over my 199, /dole pineapple. got my pancette and priscuitto. and fennel and shitake for tonites winter meal of fennel/ shitake risotto. Yum. Please send response. Do you luv*

*me ? or is this email not getting to you. I will time the
response time to see if you are in fact getting these.*

September 24, 2007

Last night I asked him why he never bought real estate
again. He says he never wanted to buy again alone and
only if he was married and said he would have done it
with me.

He said that the mom of his kids is really special but
that I was that one more special and that he wishes we
could have had a life together. I started to cry.

He also said that maybe it all works because of who he
is since he got the cancer, and it might not have been
as good if he didn't have it. I agreed that it might
be the case.

For the first time, I shared details of the conversation his mom and I had the night he checked into the
hospital for his brain tumor surgery.

I reminded him not to sit around waiting to die, but
to live as he knows he should focus on this.

We are worried about tomorrow's appointment and
Michael is more worried than he lets on.

He said that he waited all his life for me. I told
him I never thought I would find him and that it was a
miracle that I found him out of all those men listed
on the dating website.

I reminded him that early in the year he was just
hoping to make it to now and he has. He will get to
see his Alexandra's birthday in mid-October. I told

him to think about celebrating his 54th birthday and where we will be travelling then.

He says he hopes he does not ruin anyone's Christmas as he is fearful he will not live to see the rest of the year. I am fearful as well.

I said to him that should the tumor growth slow down, we should reassess and make plans.

Death is much more in the forefront as my mom's brother died suddenly of a massive heart attack earlier this month. Life is really short, so go get what you want, now.

> *From: Michael*
> *To: Cynda*
> *Date: Friday, September 28, 2007 12:31 PM*
> *Subject: as i wait*
>
> *As I wait here with baited breath wondering if I'll get mail from my sweetee. I send her sweet nothings constantly, but to no avail. I wait here all by my lonesome.*
> *I miss you, but I know I will see you first thing in the morning. We can go to Tomatos for Mexican eggs [huevos rancheros].*
> *Love hearing from you. BF xxxooxxoo*

> *From: Michael*
> *To: Cynda*
> *Date: Monday, October 1, 2007 7:35 AM*
> *Subject: wishing today goes well*
>
> *Hi Honey Bunny,*
>
> *Sorry for you ruff sleep last nite. The crampys were coming from the dead ! I hope you were able to have a small nappie whilst on your way to work. Im going to try to*

*rest before the phone rings. Im sure the community nurse
and the Kwok [Last name of his friend] will cal around the
9 zone.*

*Pleeze send email, as I wait here with baited breath for
messages from anybody out there in e-land. Maybe I
should have a blog page. It seems like my internet is
working better.*

I love you and miss you already honey pie.

BF.aka MC xxxxxxooooxxx

From: Cynda
To: Michael
Date: Monday, October 1, 2007 8:38 AM
Subject: Loving You

Honey:

*Thinking about a world without you hurts like hell. Letting
you into my world and trusting you the way I have was a
huge risk for me and my heart. I haven't let anyone in for
years because of past hurts but you are the one and it
was and has been so easy for me to let you be part of my
world. It has all come so naturally.*

*I know you do everything you can to make my life wonder-
ful and you worry and fret about things. I always appreciate everything you do and I hope you always know that.*

*I often have questioned why now that I find you and also
question why it might be much shorter than we both
deserve. Then I think that everything happens for a reason
and we have been destined to meet now because the time
is right. As much as some days it is really tough, the joy
and love are worth it.*

*Like I said last night that is why I am so sad sometimes.
There is no other Michael out there. I know that in my
heart. You are the one I have been waiting for all my life.*

*I knew so soon after meeting you that you are the man
for me.*

*I read something that really says it all:
"To the world you may be just one person, but to one
person you may be the world." - Brandi Snyder
You are my world. You and my kids that is.
No matter what happens I am always here for you.
Please continue to think about a future. Plan for
Halloween, Jake and Elwood, Christmas, New Year's, our
one year anniversary, your bd, mine and next summer, etc.
Believe in miracles because they do happen. We
deserve it.*

*I love you more than you know.
Cynda
XOXOXO*

October 6, 2007

We had Thanksgiving at my sister Crystal's house.
Michael brined and roasted the turkey. The turkey was
such a huge hit we had virtually no leftovers.

**In keeping with the cooking skills I gained from Michael, now whenever I
make a turkey, I brine it first and follow his notes.**

October 8, 2007

We celebrated Thanksgiving with my sons, Michael's
family and some Asian exchange students at his parent's home.

October, 2007

We are thinking about more travel and it is just a
matter of where and what is affordable.

Life has settled back into a routine and Michael is
cooking again, and more importantly enjoying eating.
I have been at my place a bit more as I needed to be
with my sons. Once again, it is a real struggle for me
as I miss not being with Michael especially keeping
in mind the time that is left, but I need to be a mom
as well.

After everything that I have experienced this year
since meeting Michael, I finally understand my Dad.
When my eldest was young and needed rides to hockey
or I needed help from my dad and he was reluctant, I
thought he was selfish. Now I have realised that time
is precious and as you get older you treasure it much
more as you never know when your time on this earth is
up. When you are young you feel like you have all the
time in the world to do everything that you want to
do. As you get older you realise that is no longer the
case. By my Dad not helping, it did not mean that he
did not love us, he was just making sure he had time
for what he wanted to do.

This year my life has been turned upside down and in a
good way, not a bad one. For too many years all I did
was work so hard. I worked so much overtime and all of
that money went to more things for the home, provided
my sons with more things and me with more clothes and
shoes than I can use in a lifetime. I went overboard
because I had spent so many years of being deprived. I
was so overweight for so long because I didn't think I
deserved to be happy and healthy. I had been hurt and
abused for so long that I hid behind the fat where it
was safe.

I have sacrificed so much. I slept in the living room
of a one bedroom condo for five years so that we could

get into the real estate market. I would never have been able to buy the townhouse later if I had not made the sacrifice of buying the condo first. Some family members and friends told me I was crazy and that I should just forget about the condo until I could afford a two bedroom. My gut told me that if I waited too long to buy, that I might never be able to afford a place, so I took the chance and sacrificed my comfort to provide a better life for my sons. After leaving Jeremy's father I did not date or have any interest in being involved with anyone until 2006. It had been years of loneliness but I needed to focus on being a good mom and raising my sons. Besides it was not like I had any spare time or energy.

Meeting and falling in love with Michael is the best, happiest and the saddest thing that has ever happened to me.

My little family was having a tough time as I had never been with anyone but their fathers. My sons never had to share me with anyone for 14 years.

Michael and I have something really special that I never thought I would find in my lifetime and we are grateful for it. That is why it is so important to spend as much time together as possible. I continue to hope and pray that a miracle will happen and that I will get to have a lifetime with him. I have never loved anyone or been cherished this way before. I feel certain that I will never find anyone or anything like this again in my life.

Every minute that I spend with Michael is meaningful. I treasure the silent moments, the mundane ones and the deep ones spent talking about life and death.

We know how lucky we have been to find each other and I truly believe it is all meant to be. That he was sent to me and me to him for a special reason.

If we met at some other time I don't think things would be the same or have worked. I am a very different person now than I was before I lost 94 pounds. That changed my life. I am not just a mom but also a woman and I need now, finally to put me first as life is short and I don't know how long I will have.

It was a very difficult time with my sons as well as they were angry at my not being at home for them. What choice did I have? Was I wrong to want some happiness for myself after all this time alone? They will grow up and move on to have their own lives.

October 19, 2007

We were excited to be going away for the weekend. Michael had booked a one night stay at the Rosario Resort Spa located on Orcas Island, part of the San Juan Islands.

Ironically, later that day a small plane crashed into a Richmond apartment building located about a block from Michael's place called Rosario Gardens. At the time of the accident we were already in Anacortes spending the night.

After taking the ferry to Anacortes we walked up and down the streets. We wandered leisurely in and out of many antique stores. Getting away from daily responsibilities made us forget for a brief time that soon enough life would not be so carefree.

We checked into a charming place with super comfy beds called The Marina Inn where in the evenings guests were treated to freshly baked cookies.

That night we had dinner at a quaint Thai restaurant located in a house that made you feel like you were in someone's living room.

After dinner we ventured a little further by car and went to the casino which was fun. The downside was you could still smoke in the casinos and it was pretty smoky and so we didn't stay for too long.

It had been over 20 years since I had last been to Anacortes, and although I had nothing but fond memories, the chance to return had not come up.

The next day we would board another ferry to go to Orcas Island. The Rosario Resort Spa was exactly what we needed, a beautiful tranquil setting. We enjoyed our stay and soon enough it was time to head back to reality.

October 21, 2007

It was another Chu family gathering, this time to celebrate Alexandra and Asia's birthdays as they were just days apart. Family was very important and Michael's family spent a great deal of time together.

> *From: Cynda*
> *To: Michael*
> *Date: Tuesday, October 23, 2007 9:57 AM*
> *Subject: Morning Mr. Flet*
>
> *Hi Honey:*

Hope you are dozing. Thanks for making me toast and egg. Sorry I bit off more than I can chew. I tend to do that. So do you by the way. Sometimes I think you are a bookend to me.

I know you are struggling with way too much right now and the issues with my boys doesn't help. I love you so much for being there for me and them.

I am very worried about you and so you can't tell me not to be. I know you put on a brave face and try to be strong for everyone but I need you to always be real with me. No matter how tough or how scared or how much it might hurt, I need the real you always.

I don't know why I am snoring so much. Grinding my teeth, I know why. I am doing all I can (at least while conscious) to fix it all, okay.

...

Love u
Cynda
xoxoxox

From: Michael
To: Cynda
Date: Tuesday, October 23, 2007 9:57 AM
Subject: Re: Morning Mr. Flet

Okay honey see you after. can't wait.

From: Michael
To: Cynda
Date: Wednesday, October 24, 2007 12:46 PM
Subject: Re: Are u there?

*Everything is okay sweetee. I love you very much. You
never have to ever worry that I don't love you. This is
not true at all. It never turns off. Its always in on the "ON"
position. Sometimes it gets a little sticky and on grumpy
position, but only for a minute.
I love you sweetee pot pie. Don't ever doubt it.
Love BF {a very happy guy}*

*From: Michael
To: Cynda
Date: Friday, October 26, 2007 8:12 AM
Subject: Brand New mail #1*

*Hi Honey Pie.
Hopefully you were well rested today not to sleep thru
ride to work and you are alert little bunny. By the way I am
working on the bunny food for you for dinner. Well darn if
I havent started eating those Frito corn chips. ,,,theyre so
addictive. and beautifully crunchy. yummy.*

*WE HAVE TO GO AWAY SOON ! I'M ALREADY
GETTING ANTSY TO GO AGAIN SOMEWHERE.
It doesnt have to be far. Anyway hoping to see immediate
email results sweetee. Take it easy today, mouses are
gone right. Let it all go...*

[Michael referred to "bunny food" as I was trying to eat more greens. His reference to "mouses are gone" he meant "cats are away" as bosses were away.]

October 31, 2007

On Halloween afternoon, Michael picked me up from the 29th Avenue Skytrain station [rapid transit system in Metro Vancouver, British Columbia]. I was dressed as a vampire, a sexy one of course, otherwise why do it. (I also jokingly said I was dressed as a lawyer/

litigator and that got laughs.) Michael was dressed as a pirate. Unfortunately, I neglected to get a picture of him all dressed up but I will forever remember him dressed that way. He looked so cute, wearing the pirate hat, the hook for his hand and he held a sword and goblet. It wasn't until we went back to my house that I found the eye patch which he then wore as well but I couldn't find the earring.

We went to my house to give out candy to the kids in the neighborhood. Michael happily gave out candy and chatted to the kids. The candy was in a bowl with a moving and talking hand. He brought out some fireworks, bottle rockets, I think and gave a package to Jeremy and some to Andrew as well. He was going to set some off at Rob Kwok's place but in the end gave those to Andrew. Michael was setting them off in my backyard and Mercury was one unhappy kitty while he was doing this.

We nearly ruined our dinner by snacking on leftovers and too many Halloween chocolates and candies. We stashed a pile of chocolate bars and Starburst candies in the glove compartment of Michael's car.

After giving out candies/chocolates for about an hour, we handed the bowl over to Andrew and headed over to his friend Rob's house for the yearly Halloween pasta dinner. This Halloween dinner was another milestone for Michael as he never expected to still be here. We were all so grateful.

Although Michael and I had only been together for nine months, we had already travelled to Gibsons, the Sunshine Coast, Cuba, Victoria, Brooke Valley, Dominican Republic, Orcas Island and twice to Anacortes. We

both loved to travel and wanted to get in as much while Michael was healthy enough. So far we have been lucky.

He told me that earlier that day his mom asked him if marrying me was something he considered and he told her definitely yes. Four years ago he would have for sure. She said that she thought so. She said that I am a good woman and come from a good family. He says that he told her all about the two boys, their separate fathers, the history as well as how tough it was raising two sons mostly on my own.

I was really glad that he talked to his mom about this and that she knew the extent of our feelings for each other. I told him that his mom's approval was most important to me especially if we should get married.

I felt a great deal of euphoria at hearing about this conversation. Although we have bad days, there are many good ones and I would never want to be anywhere but by his side.

Later that evening at Rob's house, Rob said to me that he and Baree talked about Michael and wondered why we had to meet so late in Michael's life and why not earlier. It was always important to me that his friends and especially his family knew that I was committed to Michael and would always be at his side.

November 1, 2007

We took in an exhibit of origami that my brother-in-law was part of at the Pendulum Gallery. Doing normal things made life less scary.

For Michael, Love Cynda

November 2, 2007

We went back to Anacortes for another weekend getaway as we enjoyed our first trip so much. It was tougher on Michael at this point with the driving. When I look back in hindsight now, it was not the smartest thing to do. He kept dozing off while we were waiting in busy traffic on the return trip. I was anxious about getting back to Vancouver safely.

November 4, 2007 in the middle of the night

During the middle of the night, Michael said to me that Mr. Flet loves Mrs. Flet so much. He was holding me really tight and hugging me. He made some comments about marriage.

He also said that he was feeling afraid as his breathing was more difficult of late and that he wasn't feeling so well. I think he also said more than once that something was wrong with him. I think he may actually have been crying as well. I am not sure as I was exhausted and only half awake. When he said that he was afraid I became more alert and did say to him that I think that the current troubles might be related to his weight gain. Also that eating fried foods may irritate his throat and therefore cause him to cough more. Anyways we did discuss health issues in Anacortes. I said I would really like him to give up deep fry and sugar for one month.

November 7, 2007

We had dinner with golfing friends at The Bavarian Haus in New Westminster. It was tough to find balance, making time to see family, see my sons and spend time at my place, Michael's friends, my friends, work

full-time, exercise and if I am lucky, get a good
night's sleep.

> *From: Michael*
> *To: Cynda*
> *Date: Wednesday, November 7, 2007 9:01 AM*
> *Subject: message 1*
>
> *hi honey, this is first message. dinner was good yesterday.*
> *did we go to bed right away.*
> *must have been tired again. were gettin older now. Oh*
> *well looks like we live for the wkends now. I got a great*
> *borscht but wondering when we will get to try it. i cant wait*
> *to spend the weekend for ourselves again. we can make*
> *tay tay too you knowl *It all takes organization and time.*
> *cramps are subsiding a bit today, we'll see. Need to hear*
> *for my honey, I miss her big time. whats the exact plan*
> *tonite. Can you let me no so theres no confusion.*
> *Love and miss you*
> *BF hurry hurry, curry in a hurry*

Michael sent me the following email and the font of the text was so large
it filled an 8 ½ x 11 sheet of paper. I carried a well worn and wrinkled
version in my wallet for a very long time.

> *From: Michael*
> *To: Cynda*
> *Date: Friday, November 16, 2007 4:01 PM*
> *Subject: I always care about you.*
>
> *I Love you So Much*
> *Honey,*
> *No matter what time and*
> *when it is.*
>
> *You never ever have to*
> *worry, cause I'm always*

just goofin around and
razzin ya bout' things,
cause I just plain love
you 100% of the time.
It's never less than that.

November 18, 2007

We were able to finally arrange a get together with some of my friends and we made pizza. Unfortunately, it ended up being stressful as the friends that we went to, knew we were making pizza but they didn't have an oven in their stove. Fortunately, we were able to bake the pizza in the neighbors' oven.

From: Cynda
To: Michael
Date: Wednesday, November 21, 2007 9:13 AM
Subject: Hi

Honey:

Got here okay. Stood almost the entire way. Sorry about the alarm clock. 1 had a bad sleep and so when that happens I don't hear the alarm. Sorry about the bathroom fan and light. I really thought I had turned off both.

I am broken right now. I am hurting really badly. I blew last night because I can't take it right now. I am very strong, but this year I have been knocked off my feet with extreme sadness as well as intense happiness (with you). It has been the toughest year of my life. Right now I need comfort and can't handle any adversity. I hate fighting with you. It breaks me.

I have to look after me and so that is what I am going to do. I have yet another canker sore this morning. That is why I am going to take an hour for me and go to the gym after work. I need to take care of me.

I am also thinking that I will run this Sat am with Abby, Harriet and Emma as Abby can't the first week in December and I cannot the second week. I haven't yet decided but think it is a good possibility.

I love u

Cynda
xoxox

From: Michael
To: Cynda
Date: Wednesday, November 21, 2007 10:02 AM
Subject: Re: Hi

Hi Honey,
Just woke at 943 and I may have heated up wrong bun. it was right in front and might be a chicken one, OH NO did u take one, or ??

From: Michael
To: Cynda
Date: Friday, November 23, 2007 3:25 PM
Subject: is it going the Allan Lim way ?

Hi Sweetee,
I hope youre having an ok day. The Allan Lim way. Go with it. Let it Go. It will soon be over. Mail me , I miss u

[Allan Lim is my brother-in-law. He would say you have to just let things go and not to hang on to it when it wasn't good for you. Michael liked this about Allan and called it "The Allan Lim way".]

November 25, 2007

Michael and I had dinner with his parents and children at the Quilchena Golf and Country Club.

> *From: Michael*
> *To: Cynda*
> *Date: Tuesday, November 27, 2007 7:45 AM*
> *Subject: take it easy today honey*
>
> *Hi, hope you arrived ok. Remember you had lots of sleep. And it allows you to live the ALLAN LIM WAY. Go with the flow, no defending required. (Its like when you don't want me to respond to a guy in the car – just let it go) I am experiencing very low inputs of emails from yu. pls send. miss them.*
> *Any sugg for dinner?*
> *Miss you already, what time you leaving today ?*
> *Love you more than everything in the whole wide world.*
> *BF xxxooooxxxxoxox*

[When Michael says "Its like when you don't want me to respond to a guy in the car – just let it go" this was when someone in traffic annoyed him and he was ready to get into an altercation.]

> *From: Michael*
> *To: Cynda*
> *Date: Tuesday, November 27, 2007 1:23 PM*
> *Subject: 30yrs*
>
> *Was talking to my mom, she says you are the best woman ever for her son and we should have been together 30 yrs ago. She says then things would have been great. But we can't dwell on that, we can cherish every moment we get together. Hope your aerobics and lunch was good. Off to Khatib soon*

December 1, 2007

We had dinner at the home of his long time friends, Cynthia and Kenny. They were very easy to like as they were both kind and warm people. Cynthia told me of the all the times that Michael had told her how lonely he was, and how he hoped to find a partner to share his life with.

From: Cynda
To: Michael
Date: Tuesday, December 4, 2007 8:44 AM
Subject: RE: have an easy day

Love u. Thanks for whispering sweet reassurances all night.
We are so lucky.

From: Michael
To: Cynda
Date: Tuesday, December 4, 2007 10:35 AM
Subject: RE: have an easy day

your welcome sweetee. I just got up now to make some breakfast. talk to you after. hope youre having a nice day.

From: Cynda
To: Michael
Date: Wednesday, December 5, 2007 8:24 AM
Subject: RE: las dec 18

Honey:
Can you do both? Vegas this month and then another trip at the beginning of January?
I can withdraw a bit of RRSP to travel in January and I want to use the opportunity to travel. I haven't and am unlikely to have this type of time off again since it has

been some 16 years since I was off for more than 10
business days.
Let me know asap... We could leave for Vegas on the 19th
of December and then come back on the 23rd.
I love you so much. You and I meeting are a miracle.
We need to see past the mundane and savour all the
wonderfulness of our lives.
"We can do anything we want to do if we stick to it long
enough." - Helen Keller

From: Michael
To: Cynda
Date: Wednesday, December 5, 2007 8:47 AM
Subject: RE: las dec 18

Hi honey, this all sounds good, but i think it will just
cost me too much money. My proirities were rings first.
travel seems very far away. We could go, but nothing to
spend. I'll think about it. Matt also offered to take me to
QCharlottes to steelhead in the mid of Jan. (Still tent)

Anyway Honey Pot Pie,

You realize that I love you every moment of the day. So
thru thick and thin, I love you each and every minute. talk
to you later.

Love BF - gpbfeaem/ ["gpbfeaem/" is "glamor pussy's best
friend for each and every minute"]

From: Cynda
To: Michael
Date: Wednesday, December 5, 2007 9:06 AM
Subject: RE: las dec 18

Honey:
I can take some money out of my RRSP for January trip

if need be, okay? I have already thought about that and would do so in order for us to travel. As I said last night I would much rather travel in January and skip vegas but if you want, we could manage to do both.
I can also work for John a couple more times in January as well.

I am so glad that rings are priority as I cannot wait (trying to be patient) to be engaged/married to you.

I know you were talking to Matt about fishing and that would be great if you can make the trip with Matt as I intend to spend a little time with Abby and getting fit in January as well.

I love you through thick and thin as well as you are my soulmate and I would be lost without you. I love you the way Hector's wife loves him (in Troy).
What does "gpbfeaem" mean? Glamour Pussy, Big Fred ....?

Big kiss
Cynda
xoxox

From: Michael
To: Cynda
Date: Wednesday, December 5, 2007 12:40 PM
Subject: RE: las dec 18

glamor pussy's best friend for each and every minute

From: Michael
To: Cynda
Date: Sunday, December 9, 2007 7:47 AM
Subject: im sorry honey pot pie

I'm so sorry honey, I should have said "fiance" or partner. Please forgive me

From: Cynda
To: Michael
Date: Sunday, December 9, 2007 8:08 AM
Subject: RE: im sorry honey pot pie

well, I toggle between partner and boyfriend for you all the time but usually go with partner
You aren't my fiance yet and I love u so much

From: Michael
To: Cynda
Date: Sunday, December 9, 2007 7:48 AM
Subject: 4 wow

That's 4 emails already before 8 am. WOW ,

BF sure loves his honey pot pie/

From: Michael
To: Cynda
Date: Sunday, December 9, 2007 7:50 AM
Subject: what was in the wash {Domestic question}

does it all go in the dryer ?

5th email

From: Michael
To: Cynda
Date: Sunday, December 9, 2007 7:57 AM
Subject: windows live

I'm on here most of time, Just nudge (ring a ding ding - 3rd one over in emoticon section) I miss you. I am going back to rest for awhile. If you phone, .. thats okay. I always will want to talk to you honey.

Any ideas for dinner yet. It feels like its all on my shoulders. ...."put your head on my shoulders" oo oo oo . babeeeeeee oo oo - paul anka.

From: Michael
To: Cynda
Date: Sunday, December 9, 2007 8:02 AM
Subject: Re: oh no

Oh no Honey pot pie.

I noticed that it's snowing outside. Is it like that at your end of the planet ???

Better let me know. This could influence our decision about this evening if it continues and grows up to be a real storm. Please let me know by phone ASAP...(not meant to be a panic issue.... relax like Allan Lim would .....go with the flow)

December 9, 2007

We had a family dinner with Michael's parents and both sets of kids at Congee Noodle King. I invited my parents as well, but was not able to get a hold of them in time.

December 13, 2007

Michael and I were going to Hawaii in January. I booked our flights rights after work today.

This evening Michael gave me an engagement ring but was so cheeky he refused to ask me the question. The diamond ring he had given me for my birthday was supposed to be "the ring" but again he didn`t ask me the question.

Earlier we had gone to see Lawrence who we had previously bought jewellery from in the summer of 2007. He had a ring for me that Michael wanted to buy but needed me to see it and try it on to confirm that it was the one.

Unbeknownst to Michael I had already fallen for this ring the first time I saw it which was in the summer of 2007. I had priced it at that time and it was significantly more than I had money for. I had really wanted to buy a bracelet which is what I did at that time. I also bought a pinkie ring for Michael that had a hummingbird on it. I now often wear that ring on my middle finger on my right hand and think of him when I look at it.

The ring was perfect. I have always preferred white gold or silver over yellow gold. The ring was silver with a white gold setting holding the stone. The stone happened to be an aquamarine which was Michael's birthstone. Michael had hoped to get me a ring with a red stone as I didn't have a red one and had been thinking about getting one.

I told him I far preferred the aquamarine as it was a very pale blue and almost translucent and more importantly it was Michael's birthstone. As he often said things just come to us naturally and easily. Once again this was the case. It all just fell into place easily and simply.

Later I found out that Aquamarine is a stone of courage. I liked that as Michael was the most courageous man I had ever met.

I bought Michael`s ring from Lawrence on December 13th. Lawrence was at a jewellery show somewhere downtown that day. Lawrence was selling us a custom made ring that someone no longer wanted. It had mountain ranges on it, Grouse, Seymour and Cypress with a sun and was in gold and silver. It was perfect for Michael as he used to ski and was a ski instructor when he was younger.

Dec 14/07

Ebasing - Comittment
Ring - Engage
to Cynda

Michael December 14, 2007 [actually Dec.13, 2007] Journal Entry

December 16, 2007

Michael has booked a condo for two weeks. Staying at the Makaha Valley Towers located in Waianae. Yay!!

December 18/07 (Tues)

Been Floundering on what to do with this journal.

Thought I'd continue with our Hawaian 2 wk Trip to come Jan 1st

So glad Bee is coming. Wish Eric was as agonised but school, age, etc.

Off to CClinic today, first time in 2 months. Hope things are okay. Need refills.

Feeling okay, strength less I rate about 70-75% steroids effect. Hair 60% return so far.

Still considering golf clubs to go

Will check with handy Bird about Car insur. abroad.

Michael December 18, 2007 Journal Entry

CHAPTER NINE
PLAYING IN A DIFFERENT SANDBOX

December 19, 2007

Today was my last day at my job. I had been contemplating leaving this position before I met Michael and now I had quit in order to have some extra time to spend with him.

Here is my farewell speech given in the boardroom:

Thank you for everyone who was able to take the time out to see me off.

Thanks for the kind words and the great gift. I will appreciate it when we are away.

The following is what I said in the boardroom and is reproduced for those of you who didn't make it, or are away.

It is important to me that I share this with you.

Wow, I cannot believe I am actually leaving. I always joked that when I won the lottery I would retire and leave. As sappy as it sounds, I do feel like I have won the lottery, personally that is.

Although, I can be very private, I can also be quite candid. I am passionate about what I care about and I know it's my downfall. Caring too much is not always good, it can hurt you, but then I am not good at not being me. Those of you who have known me for years have received my emails soliciting donations for yet another cause.

It seems fitting that I am leaving at the end of 2007 as it has been an amazing year for me. In January I met my soul mate (they really do exist) who is now my fiancé/husband. He proposed on December 13th and we exchanged rings to formalise our commitment. With Michael I have travelled more in one year than I have in my entire life. We have been to Cuba and the Dominican Republic as well some shorter trips to Victoria, the Sunshine Coast, San Juan Islands and Anacortes. In August he took me and my sons to his family's private lake, up north, just outside of Brooke Valley where I caught not only my first fish, but 6 subsequent fish. Talk about highs.....On January 1st we leave for Hawaii to lay on the beach for two weeks.

Life is very short and there is an expression that goes "Life is not measured by the breaths you take, but by the moments that take your breath away – Vicki Corona.". That is a mantra that I have been trying to live by this year. In 2007 I have done more things for me than I have in my life. Everyone should make and take time to look after themselves. Ask yourself who suffers if you don't. There is another expression. "Work to live and not live to work."

This year I attended an unprecedented three funerals. Two were for older uncles, and one hit home particular hard. He was my sister's brother-in-law. He died in an accident at age 47. It makes you think.

So reflect on this past year and take the chance to do something different. Don't wait for some day. It may never come and before you know it life might just pass you by. Learn to do something new, take that class, learn that sport, lose those 10 lbs, get fit, and change your life. Give yourself that something you have always wanted and just put off.

I am saying all of this to you because I care. I have been lucky enough to work with some of the nicest people in town. That is what they always say about Stikeman. It's the people and it truly is.

I have really enjoyed being a part of the Litigation Department. Working for Gordon has definitely been the challenge I was seeking years ago. I have learned so much and I have really enjoyed the work.

So why am I leaving? A very wise lady lawyer, now a Judge of the Provincial Court once said to me, sometimes you just want to play in a different sandbox. Although it won't be the same as being here, I will keep in touch. You are all going to be missed.

That evening we had dinner with Sam and Lana at Paesanos, an Italian restaurant with an Indian chef located in Richmond. One of their specialties was Bombay Penne.

Dec 20 /07

I have learned that I can spend a lot of time by myself, but I love being with Cynda. She is definitly my other perspective.

- Getting a bit concerned about cash. Need to figure out something or win lotto. I'll take latter for Cynda & I.

I sure am enjoying the xmas music this year. So happy to be given Christmas this yr.

Michael December 20, 2007 Journal Entry

Christmas 2007

I had decided that after spending Christmas Eve with Michael and the boys at my house, that I would return to his place and spend the night there. It was really important for me to do so as it may be our only Christmas together. Considering Michael never expected to see summer 2007, we never dreamed we would be fortunate enough to have Christmas and we were so grateful he was still here.

On Christmas Eve it is tradition at my home to watch a new movie after dinner. Dinner was usually appetizers and then we would watch the movie. This year I had chosen the movie Ratatouille. Michael, as expected, made a fuss about watching a kid's movie. In the end it was a huge hit with him and he couldn't stop telling everyone what a great movie it was. His enthusiasm was boundless and when something made him excited he wanted to share it with the world. This pure joy and passion of his made me love him even more. He couldn't believe how much he enjoyed the movie and I reminded him that I had told him he would.

Michael's family's tradition was breakfast Christmas morning at his parents. He recreated the enormous breakfast that we shared in Anacortes. Ingredients comprised of eggs, hash browns, corned beef, green onions and cheese, lots of cheese.

Cousins from Vancouver Island and elsewhere came to his parents and it a day full of blessings.

Later that day I went with my sons to my parents for dinner and Michael joined us later that evening.

December 27, 2007

I was still not feeling well as I had gotten sick just before Christmas. I was taking antibiotics due to some kind of infection. I always got nervous about getting sick as Michael's immune system was compromised and I never wanted him to catch a cold or virus. He never wanted me to go home when I got sick, but insisted on taking care of me at a risk to his own health.

December 31, 2007

We celebrated New Year's Eve at the home of a golfing couple, Maisie and Thomas. Sam and Lana were there as well. It was an evening of good fun and laughter, another unexpected blessing.

January 1, 2008

Today we were leaving for Hawaii and we were as free as
could be. I had left my job shortly before Christmas
and didn't have a new job yet, but would look for one
once we returned from Hawaii. The job market was currently incredible and I couldn't have picked a better
time to be job hunting.

As I had the time with me not working, we would be
going for two whole weeks. I had never before taken
a vacation for that long nor had Michael. Alexandra
would be coming with us for the first week and then we
would have a second week alone. Unfortunately, due to
school Eric was not able to come with us.

Michael and I flew out on WestJet at 6:30 pm. Alexandra
was coming on a separate flight and was arriving around
the same time as us. We would meet up at the airport
and then go to pick up our rental car, a comfortable SUV.

Michael drove us from Waikiki to our rented condo in
Makaha, north of Waikiki, on the West side of the
Island of Oahu and about an hour away. It was very
dark and driving there wasn't a problem as we had
very clear directions from the owner of the condo. We
stopped to buy bottled water to drink and then again
at McDonald's to get some hamburgers to eat. We were
all quite hungry as it had been several hours since we
had last eaten.

We arrived at the condo around 1:00 am and fell into
bed pretty quick as we were beat. The next morning
when we woke up to intense sun, we looked out the
windows and it was like a scene out of the movie

Jurassic Park. We were surrounded by lush, green mountains and at any moment I expected the dinosaurs to come out. Our location was incredible and the view was spectacular. It was 25°C and it couldn't get more beautiful than this, we were truly in paradise.

We were told by neighbors that it wasn't usually so green on the mountain, but lots of rain earlier in the year made it so. Wild boars and billy goats lived on the mountain but we never saw them.

The complex was a gated community and the grounds were lush, full of tropical flowers as well as about 20 peacocks, at least as many cats as well as a mongoose, what a treat it was to see them.

We bought our groceries in Waianae at a local family owned grocery store, Tamura Super Market, as they sold a large variety of items. We were able to buy ahi tuna, meat, fish and deli items like poke [a raw meat/fish appetizer in Hawaiian cuisine] and wakame seaweed salad. Because we were staying in a condo, we cooked and ate there much of the time. We also bought fresh mangos, ripened in the Hawaiian sun, from a vendor on the side of the road. I did laundry, Michael cooked, and we played house.

From: Mae
To: Cynda
Date: Sunday, January 6, 2008 11:55 AM
Subject: WestJet travel itinerary. Have a great flight!

Thanks for writing, I am always worried as to how Michael is doing and that he is not doing too much, afterall I think you guys really like the warmth. Have a great time and good flight home. It is sleeting outside and cold.

Baree asked if we heard from you. It is surprising but Michael should know that his brother also worries about him, All the bitching he does is sometimes intolerable and yet we know that he is ours.
That's unquestionable love ahe Michael. Mom
Happy New Year and Dick & I thank you cynda.

This trip and time with Michael was magical. Although we had some disagreements, we also played a lot and had fun. We were a normal couple doing normal things. On one occasion we were lying on the grass at a park and taking silly selfies of ourselves. It was also special that Alexandra was with us as I got to know her better. It wasn't an easy time for his family and they had welcomed me with open arms.

Cynda and Michael Selfie in Hawaii

I can still feel the warmth and remember everything so vividly. I went for runs and walks many mornings, and took advantage of the perfect weather.

Once when we were walking along the beach, he commented that it would be nice to get married in Hawaii.

Although I had been to Hawaii twice before, there was so much I had yet to experience which I was getting to do now. We lunched on enormous shrimp at Fumi's Kahuku Shrimp truck and went to the world famous Matsumoto for shaved ice. We also stopped in a few quaint, old fishing towns. A couple of trips to the Aloha Stadium for their swap meet where I bought a dress, Alexandra bought a bikini and Michael a Hawaiian shirt. Michael already had quite the collection of Hawaiian shirts, and it grew during this trip.

We logged a great deal of mileage as we travelled from Makaha to downtown Waikiki and all around the island. Michael golfed with Alexandra as well as with a Rob Kwok who was vacationing there at the same time. We had dinner with a friend and his wife who lived there, as well as many lazy days lying on the beach.

We watched the sun sink into the horizon on many evenings, and we were in awe. It was one of the most memorable and beautiful sights.

Another happy event for Michael was going to visit Malu, a woman who he had met on his first trip to Hawaii in 2006. She had also had cancer but had won her battle. It was so nice to meet her and she gave him a Waikiki Beach Boy t-shirt which he wore all the time.

I contacted Malu after he died and she posted a heartfelt message to his online obituary.

Michael's health was definitely deteriorating. As much as he was thriving being in Hawaii, the warmth and heat being a much needed panacea, he was having a tougher time breathing and was gasping for air. Now, he really needed daily naps. He was also very stubborn and would push himself and insisted on doing all the driving for the entire trip. I never learned to drive as it made me nervous, and although Alexandra could drive, he never asked her to.

January 16, 2008

Back to reality, we returned to Vancouver from Hawaii late in the evening.

January 19, 2008

I went with Michael to see his palliative care doctor, Dr. Clark Khatib. He reviewed Michael's symptoms as well as his current course of medication.

Michael told the doctor that breathing was becoming more difficult. The doctor prescribed the use of oxygen to help him to breathe. It was tough for him to admit to needing the oxygen, but over time the benefits out-weighed his reluctance.

January 20, 2008

Today is the one year anniversary of our first date, an anniversary I never dreamed I would get to share with Michael. I am grateful as well as afraid. I know I should just take one day at a time.

> *From: Cynda*
> *To: Michael*
> *Date: Monday, January 21, 2008 9:50 AM*
> *Subject: Morning*
>
> *Hi Dear:*
> *Hope you got some quality sleep after all. I am*

having cereal for breakfast as I type this. I am already running late.

Anyways, I will call you later.
Regarding the cleaning lady, get her to:
Clean 2 x bathrooms
vacuum
dust all the rooms
wash all the floors
clean the kitchen (sink, counters, microwave and outside of the appliances)
put on the dishwasher as well as washing up what is there.

I know you are struggling and having a tougher time of late. I cannot always fix it for you. I have to look after me too and I feel the strain lately. That is a big part of my being cranky. It's not hormones. I want to be there for you but I feel I am never there for Jeremy and Andrew.

Loving you is not easy as I know the eventual outcome won't necessarily be what I want. It is not that I don't believe in miracles but I have to be realistic too. I am struggling too as it is all new to me.
We will talk more later.
Love u
Cynda aka Sweetee Pie

From: Cynda
To: Michael
Date: Friday, January 25, 2008 10:41 PM
Subject: Big Flet

I think that BF and GP need to get together very soon as GP is suffering terribly from no BF.

For Michael, Love Cynda

February 1, 2008

We had dinner with William and Matt tonight. They had
an opportunity to spend about a month in Cancun and
invited Michael to join them. The prospect of spending time somewhere warm was enticing. He was really
torn about going as I would be starting a new job on
February 8th, and would not be able to go with him. I
told him that if he wanted, I would quit the new job
even though I did not know how I would manage financially. Michael decided not to go.

From: Michael
To: Cynda
Date: Saturday, February 2, 2008 10:17 AM
Subject: Re: Morning

*alarm at 9 but slept till 10. Feeling most refreshed I have
ever felt. Must be o2 treatments in my blood thru the last
few days. Feels like I got some energy today.*

*Send back message if chance. I will call later. dinner
at 715*

Love bf xxxxooo

Upon our return to Vancouver, I went to work part-time
for the lawyer with the home office who I had worked
for when I first met Michael. I needed some income
while I was looking for a new job.

On one occasion Michael came to pick me up after work
and charmed the lawyer so much that we left with a
bottle of wine.

February 3, 2008

Michael is doing much better since being on oxygen and is using it almost all the time. He has been able to take less medication during the day and night as he is not coughing as heavily and gasping. The downside is that the constant flow of oxygen has caused his nasal passages to dry out and he now needs to use a lubricating nasal gel.

Michael's reliance on constant oxygen was another thing to learn and I soon became adept at connecting and disconnecting the various oxygen cylinders.

At home, Michael had an oxygen concentrator which produced continuous oxygen. Although it was kept in the dining room at the opposite end of the apartment, it was noisy, and sometimes made it hard to fall asleep.

We always did our best to order extra cylinders in case of a power outage. We had an outage once and it would have meant an ambulance trip to the hospital if we did not have extra cylinders.

On a few occasions, Michael would have trouble breathing in the night. I would be startled from sleep to jump up and make sure the concentrator was on or the cylinder still contained oxygen. When he used the cylinders we had to be mindful of when it would run out of oxygen. I was frequently anxious and did not always sleep well.

That evening we had a Chinese New Year's family dinner at Mr. Ho's Wonton House with my family and Michael's son Eric and his best friend Vince.

February 4, 2008

Michael is having a tough time emotionally. He had lunch with friend Rob and then had a visit with the nurse in the afternoon. He wasn't able to rest as much as he should have. He didn't eat dinner that evening. He said he had no energy and was tired.

From: Michael
To: Cynda
Date: Monday, February 4, 2008 10:29 PM
Subject: dr appt

I have Dr Khatib appt tomorrow at 220 pm. to ask about morphine mgmt instead of tussionex. Specifically about slow action release morph. for pain. Stacey and Rainbow think that might be the way. I can also ask about swelling and resumption of Altace medication.

You have any questions for dr. khatib. Call me or email.

Love you honey pot pie. Miss you. i wish you were coming home tonite. Dinners and meals just not the same.

:love BF

From: Cynda
To: Michael
Date: Tuesday, February 5, 2008 8:19 AM
Subject: dr appt

Glad you are going to Dr. Khatib. Ask him more about the oxygen and that if you are handling things properly. (I think you are).
Also today is the day that you need to order the oxygen from Medigas. By the end of the day. My thoughts are 5 large and 4 small. What do you think?
Love you lots too.

Take it easy and remember to rest.

Cynda

xoxox

Some days after work I would hop on the Skytrain, go to T & T Supermarket, get groceries, hop back on the Skytrain and meet Michael. We always met at the 29th Avenue Skytrain station to go to my home. It was 40 minute drive from his home in Richmond to mine in Burnaby. With traffic it could be double that. He would have to nap at my home before the return trip to Richmond. As he became sicker, the drive was out of the question.

February 5, 2008

I had been staying at my place for the past while and it was tough being apart. This is the most time we have spent apart since last April. It was due to my family obligations and although Michael could have stayed at my place, I have stairs and he never stayed there as Jeremy was just a teenager, and he didn't feel it was appropriate.

I would be spending all day tomorrow with Michael and then dinner with his Dad's side of the family at Golden Swan Restaurant.

February 8, 2008

I had accepted a new legal secretarial position late January and started work today.

February 10, 2008

We celebrated Chinese New Year's with a dinner with Michael's parents and family.

February 12, 2008

A friend of Andrew's is now staying at my home to look after Jeremy and I am back at Michael's. Andrew was travelling in Asia. Last year when he was away at school in the United States, his friends were amazingly supportive and I could not have survived without the help of Carson Z., Jeff N. and Jon S.

I am constantly torn between being there for Michael and also being a parent to my sons.

> *From: Cynda*
> *To: Michael*
> *Date: Thursday, February 14, 2008 8:01 AM*
> *Subject: morning*
>
> *Love you lots Mr. Chu!!!*

> *From: Michael*
> *To: Cynda*
> *Date: Thursday, February 14, 2008 10:44 AM*
> *Subject: morning*
>
> *Happy Valentine's Day Sweetee!!!!*

February 14, 2008

I gave Michael a Valentine's Day card. I wrote about what was happening a year ago and what a miracle it is that we are having a second Valentine's Day together.

> *From: Michael*
> *To: Cynda*
> *Date: Friday, February 15, 2008 11:32 AM*
> *Subject: do we have everything*
>
> *Honey Pot Pie,*

Do we have everything to bring up to the Turners. I'm sure you will call soon anyway and hope you read this list. Did you see the money for you and you forgot your coffee. silly goose. call me sooon hunny bunny, i miss you now, its quiet ober here. I;m picking you up right?

Love GP's BF

From: Michael
To: Cynda
Date: Monday, February 18, 2008 1:14 AM
Subject: SB [South Beach diet]

Hi Honey Pot pie.
Don't worry about anything now sweetee and we will be southbeaching tonite.
And will try to stay with the program without HUMOUS.
We'll just go over and get some chick peas and sesame and tahini oil which we still may have. If not we'll get some'
We can make homemade guacamole without any foolish processed mayos in them.
I've been reading it so maybe can make super tasting food within the guidlines. I'll talk to you later or email. It takes so long for you to reply. Hurry,,,,,,huh.... huh.... hurry, hurry hurry ....(doesn't that wording just look fast and movin?
So I try my best to get things ready for you and me.!!!
I love you Hunny
Bunny.........
<love.> BF

From: Cynda
To: Michael
Date: Monday, February 18, 2008 7:59 AM
Subject: SB

Morning my silly, crazy and most adorable man.
You were so sleepy this am. I hope that you are getting a better snooze now.
No more muffins before bed.
I had a good sleep on the bus so that helps. Can't type too fast as I am still a little sleepy.
Anyways, I will leave right at 4:00 pm.
Thanks re the diet. I can't gain more weight.
I am going to probably stop and pick up your cheese slices after work. Also checking out the gym at lunch.
...
Be a good boy and rest today. Take care and drink lots of water and eat at regular times. Makes you feel better.
I will call you at lunch time.
Love u
HPP. [Honey Pot Pie]

Late this month we adopted a cat named Spyder from a local shelter. Michael never had a cat before and had grown quite fond of them after spending time with my cat Mercury, and his aunt and uncle's cat Wispy.

Having Spyder around was good for Michael's wellbeing and he was less lonely during the day. He didn't always have energy to do anything much so Spyder was the perfect companion.

Life again was smooth going for the most part, and it was back to doing routine things. There was a sense of normalcy and it was good. I was getting to the gym and to yoga, much needed exercise.

February 20, 2008

Michael has become more restless during the night
and is often awake and sits in his office or the
living room.

> *From: Michael*
> *To: Cynda*
> *Date: Wednesday, February 20, 2008 10:57 AM*
> *Subject: Happy H [Hump] Day*
>
> *just got up at 11. Feel reasonably refreshed. ate the
> oranges and on to the gai bow [chicken bun]. we'll see
> from here. I'll forward Malu's note. I love you*
>
> *MC / BF [Michael Chu/Big Flet] maybe we go out for
> dinner ?*

> *From: Michael*
> *To: Cynda*
> *Date: Friday, February 29, 2008 11:32 AM*
> *Subject: r u there everything okay*
>
> *Hi honey,*
>
> *Everything okay dwn there. Hope you had good sleep. I'm
> catching up. No dinner plan yet. Let me know. R U gyming
> or what today>?*
>
> *Love "the neglected guy" formerly BF [Big Flet]
> at least GP [Glamor Pussy] saw action recently, do
> u remember?*

> *From: Cynda*
> *To: Michael*
> *Date: Friday, February 29, 2008 4:04 PM*
> *Subject: r u there everything okay*

For Michael, Love Cynda

You are so cheeky Mr. Chu, literally that is.
Mr. BF kept dozing off. I couldn't get his attention. Must be losing my touch.
Yes, GP remembers and remembers well...
Missing you.

From: Cynda
To: Michael
Date: Sunday, March 2, 2008 10:41 PM
Subject: Tonite

Dinner was really nice and you looked really cute (I know guys don't like to be told they look cute but you did) and adorable wearing your black car coat. The coat you were wearing when I first met you and you came to my house, you know the one under the big tree.

It is great that it is March. Although some days I have a really tough time I am always glad and happy to be with you.

I know I feel much better since I have been dieting and exercising. I want to look and feel good.
Tomorrow night we should eat the broccoli and I don't know what you want for meat, maybe we could have tofu? Anyways talk to you later.
Honey Pot Pie

From: Michael
To: Cynda
Date: Monday, March 3, 2008 11:01 AM
Subject: emails

Well I've already been over to [Dr.] Khatib's office and got prescripts. I am very very tired though and will have to rest some more. It's nice to get your email < I even wrote a review for last nites dinner. I will go feed Spyder his meat

*dinner soon. Email back and phone would be nice. Okay
I love you too and miss you. We should see how things
are when you leave. Maybe can pick u up at SStore @ 5
or so. Get the clump [cat litter] and MBQ [HK BBQ Master,
a restaurant] and get outta dodge , . . unless you think it's
extra busy at that time ??*

Love Sweetee Pot Pies best friend,

Big Flet "the man"

*From: Michael
To: Cynda
Date: Tuesday, March 4, 2008 11:55 AM
Subject: Morning*

Hi Honey,

*got youre note, thank you. Dinner considerations are good.
but I thought we might have " Chiopino" instead. we Need:*

1 crab, clams,mussells, shrimps a piece of basa,

2 - 3 Ciopino sausages, 1 can lg tomatoes.

*and then we have a beautiful spanish soup bouliabase
dinner. Sour dour [dough] bread or a couple of those buns
would be good.*

Love you, miss u

BF

March 12, 2008

I had an unexpected day off today. The building I
worked in had to be closed due to a complete power
outage. I met up with Michael for his Endocrinologist
appointment. After his appointment we went to Kalvin's,

a Taiwanese restaurant for lunch. I am not sure if he was excited, tired or just no longer as good at driving as he drove up on to the curb when parking. He seemed just as surprised by this, quickly reversed, straightened the car and parallel parked.

Shortly before his 54th birthday Michael recorded a video with the help of Matt. There were two versions, one for family and one for everyone else. In the one to family he thanked all the people in his life, his parents, his children, their mother, his brother, his niece and me. He talked about childhood memories with cousins, aunts and uncles. His athletic pursuits, golf, fishing, skiing, friendships and work life.

It was a difficult thing for him to do, and such a loving and thoughtful gesture on his part. He should have been hooked up to oxygen while doing this but he chose to not use it while being recorded. Making this video took a great deal of energy from him physically and emotionally.

To me he said that I definitely understood him and that it was important that I knew how much I meant to him, that I meant everything. He worried about me having a hard time later. He reminisced about our travels and how glad it was with me and that there will be a whole lot more. He added that things seem to always work out for us and that he is really happy about that. Then he teared up and stopped talking.

He talked about "the passing". He didn't want us to mourn and grieve. He said he would likely discuss the topic of the other side with some professional with an emphasis on the word "pro". The way he said the word made me laugh.

He ended the video telling us to enjoy our lives and to live each and every moment to the best we can and that there is no other way to live. He said to try to do what you want in life and to enjoy yourself.

As I am now finishing this book, watching the CD again feels different. It no longer makes me feel so sad. Instead, I am quite surprised that it gives me comfort and makes me feel good. I have had an unexpected blow to my health lately and have been feeling defeated. After listening to Michael, I have a renewed sense of strength and believe that there is nothing I cannot overcome and nothing I cannot achieve. He always made me believe in myself when I had doubts. I remember him getting annoyed with me when I doubted myself and he would say "Where is that self-assured, confident woman that I fell in love with?"

March 22, 2008

We went to the Vedder River for a day of fishing with Eric, Vince, Ian, Matt and his girlfriend. Michael's great passions in life were golfing, fishing and food.

March 23, 2008

Baree and Molly hosted Easter dinner at their home. Our families were together and after dinner just about everyone played poker.

CHAPTER TEN
MICHAEL'S 54TH BIRTHDAY

March 26, 2008

It was Michael's 54th birthday and it was another day that he had never expected to reach.

His birthday horoscope in the local paper that day was appropriate. It said that he was more than aware of his limitations this year and not to waste time trying to do what he knew he could not succeed at. That he should put his energy into what he could accomplish. Lastly, that if he was honest about his abilities, he would find success when he focused on what was important.

For about six weeks, I had been busy preparing for his birthday. With his help, I compiled a list of guests and made arrangements to have everyone for dinner at Accents Restaurant. There would be about 50 people coming.

Michael called me a few times before the party as he very anxious that day and had an upset stomach. His preference was for me to go to Richmond and arrive at the restaurant with him. He knew that because time was tight, it made sense for me to meet him at the restaurant.

What he didn't know about his party, was that I had asked everyone to dress up in their favourite Hawaiian/tropical clothes and I had come to the restaurant earlier to decorate it. I had purchased leis, umbrella favours and Michael's favourite Chinese lucky candy (a strawberry flavoured candy) for each person's place setting.

I had also been busy creating a photo album for him for his birthday. It was filled with all the events since I had met him.

When he arrived he was so touched to see everyone. Friends and family out did themselves dressing in their best Hawaiian/tropical clothing. For some friends, like Michael's good friend William, he just wore his usual, a Hawaiian shirt. I knew without a doubt that Michael would be wearing a Hawaiian shirt.

Michael and Cynda

After dinner we had birthday cake and there were speeches. I had sent emails to friends and family of Michael's asking them to share stories.

For Michael, Love Cynda

We received an email from Malu, all the way from Hawaii, wishing him Hau'oli Makahiki Hou! (Happy Birthday).

I read out an email from his friend and former business partner Henry. He now lived in another province, and wasn't able to come out. Here is an excerpt of that email:

> Mike worked at Big Bird Sound in his early years in the audio industry, an industry that was a great love and a great provider for Mike for many years. He learned two key traits at Big Bird - how to listen to the hi-end sound; and how to sell - both of which would stand him in good stead later in his career.
>
> Mike went on to join A&B Sound when it was a real powerhouse in Southwestern BC. He became one of the all-time greatest salesmen among a cadre of great salesmen at A&B in that era. When A&B wanted to move upscale, they asked Mike to lead by becoming head buyer for the Audio Dept. Mike started bringing in the world's most prestigious brands, one of which was the coveted B&W Loudspeakers from England. That's where I met Mike. I was the Sales Rep for B&W and Mike won me over with his charm, knowledge of the hi-end, and no bull-shit way of dealing.
>
> ...
>
> Later in the evening, in that same symposium, Mike appeared to be asleep, leaned back, head tucked down, eyes closed. The facilitator asked if Mike was asleep but before anyone could move, Mike replied, "Nope. The video is shut down, but the audio is still working."
>
> Mike invents his own names for things - the Coquihalla Hwy becomes the ... Hwy; ... - immediately

understandable and very funny. He does it in the middle of a sentence.

Mike is a very spiritual person. We shared many hotel rooms over the years of travel and talked late into the night. His consciousness of a power outside himself, much greater than himself, is profound. He knows it and deals with it with great gentleness and respect, intimately.

...

Mike is much younger than me. For my 54th he bought me a bottle of Geritol and blanket for my knees. What are friends for?

I also shared his mom`s childhood stories.

When Michael was 7 years old and Baree was 5 years old, both were in bed and Baree fell asleep first.

Baree began to snore, much to Michael's dismay, as he could not get to sleep with the noise.

He did the only thing he thought was the solution to the situation. He gets up and walks over to where Baree was sleeping and he pinches his nose to close off the airway.

Well...you can guess what happened next.

(The mischievous side of Mae could not help but laugh when she found out I had a tendency to snore. Michael would not dare to pinch my nose.)

The BB gun affair. While Dick and I were shopping I told Michael and Baree that if they were going to shoot the BB gun they had strict orders to shoot it in the

basement where their Dad had created a gunny sack
filled with sand.

But no, they went out into the backyard where they
saw some birds and proceeded to shoot at them. They
managed to clear the alley and right into the huge
kitchen window pane across the alley.

Two days later - the neighbour came over and asked if
we had a BB gun. Yes, was the answer and I knew then
the kids had been outside. Needless to say, she had a
number of holes in her window.

Sam, his golfing buddy and close friend spoke and here
is an excerpt of what he said:

Lately we haven`t played as much, as you have been
battling cancer. Just like in golf you have fought this
illness with all your heart and soul. You continue to
beat the odds and I marvel at the way you`ve done
it. I was amazed to see you walk over to the waiting
room, just hours after having brain surgery. It shows
your tenacity and sisu a Finish term for determination
and your passion for life. You`ve never complained of
the unfairness of your becoming sick and looked for
whatever ways you could fight it.

From: Michael
To: Cynda
Date: Friday, April 4, 2008 10:13 AM
Subject: Re: zzzzzz

*I'm so sorry to hear you are tired. Now I wonder if you
have iron poor blood or what. I have been up since and
don't feel that bad. Not sleepy yet.
BTW was something supposed to happen at 10 this
morning? I can't remember.*

I gotta go to LD [London Drugs] to get preseriptions filled.
Maybe Que Pasa [Mexican food store in Richmond] for
some Soda Pop. Do you want anything ?
Let me know soon ok doky. Love you, miss you, we can
future shop it over here after if you want.

Love BF

From: Michael
To: Cynda
Date: Monday, April 14, 2008 3:06 PM
Subject: left over

Hi Honey Pot Pie.

Well I got up enough energy to go to Happy Dates [Happy
Date Restaurant] and have a Seu yook (crispy pork
without the crispy) /tofo rice dish with soft white tofu. It was
with mushrooms and green onions too. Yummy ooo

goo. [good]

Well I ate it with great glea and it was excellent. I had a
perfect "left over" portion put away to "take home".

I was 1/2 way home when I realized I had left my dish right
in front of my nose on the table forgeting to "take home"

What a BLOW for mankind. I feel so Stupid and robbed
of my intellect and wasn't going to return to hassle with
parking and try to find my leftover in the garbage. Do you
think this is depression? I'm such an IDIOT>

Talk to you later. Hope you get this today

His Fletness - Idiot Baron from Stupidville.

From: Cynda
To: Michael
Date: Monday, April 14, 2008 4:13 PM
Re: left over

Sweetheart, don't be so tough on yourself.
You have to remember that you are on lots of meds
and that plays havoc some days with your memory.
Considering everything I think you are amazing, except of
course when you are Mr. Cranky pants.
Okay, i love u lots.
See u soon.

April 15, 2008

Michael had an appointment at 2:50 pm with his palliative doctor, Dr. Khatib.

From: Michael
To: Cynda
Date: Friday, April 18, 2008 3:47 PM
Subject: see you when you get here

hI, hONEY pOT PIE, THIS IS a note to tell you that I love
you and you have not been forgotten, ven [even] though
you snore, we will rectify this problem for you and me
because it is an even promblem, not just yours or miside
promblem. ok Send me email before you leave.

Love BF xxxxxooo you never send anymore. [I am not
sending him emails.]

April 22, 2008

Michael's Morphine dosage was recently increased and
breathing is easier.

From: Cynda
To: Michael
Date: Tuesday, April 22, 2008 8:00 AM
Subject: My honey

Hi my honey:
Sure nice to get those hugs from you this am and the
kisses too. I know it takes a lot of energy for you to do
things. When you hug me I feel warm and gooey inside
and all is right with the world. You make me feel safe and
secure and so very loved.
Have a wonderful day. Have a nice lunch with Maisie.
Tell her I say hi. I really like her a lot. She is a very nice
person.
Cynda
...

From: Michael
To: Cynda
Date: Tuesday, April 22, 2008 8:30 AM
Subject: My honey

Honey Pot Pie,
ok honey, more energy today I guess. We can see if I
recycle the cans or not. [bring the empties to the return
depot] and if I bring the florescent bulbs out today for a
ride to Cdn Tire.

I noticed you didn't set the clock for 10:15 for Maisie. I set
it, you don't have to panic about calling.

Jeez, we havent had suchi hachei [Sushi Hachi, a
Japanese restaurant] for awhile. I talk to you later then,.
or call.

Love BGP'sF [Big Flet's Glamor Pussy] I L Y H P P/ [I love
you Honey Pot Pie]

From: Michael
To: Cynda
Date: Thursday, April 24, 2008 1:27 AM
Subject: My honey

Honey, I don't think it's correct of you to think you don't do things right.

I happen to think you do. After all you are my soul mate and you feel exactly like i do about most things.

We definitely are having a problem for you not feeling right about things. I know this has to be, because it's not my house you're living away from. You have been living at my house that your statement about feeling displaced has to be getting so true. It especially impacted when we kinda looked at "where would you [your] stuff go"

You probably don't like it, but chores for me have to going up as my energy levels allow me less possibilities at doing them. I like to think I'm getting some energy back, but each day is different and I don't have a routine really. I might be slowly getting depressed and not knowing it. After all I only spend a few hours with anyone. You are the only one I spend any significant time with but it is usually after dinner 8 to 10 = couple to 3 hrs day. So....you see I don't even get to ineract [interact] with or variety of folk and people like you do, at work. So its pretty lonely out here. You can catch up to Lost, Grey's, Private Practise, etc,

So I think a good plan is as follows. You should work your your way home most evenings now. Get "placed" again. You can come here on weekends if you like. I just want what is best for you. You sound much happier if you go settle in at your house for awhile. Maybe go there for the weekdays, come over for wkends if youre inclined. This should work sweetee pot pie. Let me know.

Spidyr [Spyder] and I will figure it out thru the week.

Love, BF Mr. Flet himself. the one and only.

From: Michael
To: Cynda
Date: Thursday, April 24, 2008 5:22 AM
Subject: last letter

The getting back in order letter is such a poorly written letter. I realized after reading it a couple of hrs later. You'll have to sift thru it carefully and you get the words I'm sure.

The bottom line was that I don't spend much time with anybody and am becoming very crankypanty.

Mr. Crankypanty is having a hard time getting along with anyone nowadays. I think its probably because of my condition is tougher to soothe. I think I hurt just a little bit more.

Thanks for the Noodles, can steam for snack/lunch.

Would sure like to go to Zellers ? and get some suspenders or if you see along the way can you pick up. They should be at least 2 inches wide(er) Red ones okay, blue, just a manly color, just not rainbow colored. I can pay you back for them if you find. If not we can go tonite and find. We should bring the bulbs back to Cdn Tire too. Love you sweetee pot pie.

BF xxxxoooxxx

Email or phone

From: Cynda
To: Michael
Date: Thursday, April 24, 2008 8:09 AM
Subject: Re: last letter

I can't imagine how tough life is for you some days. I try and I sympathize and try to do everything I can to make you comfy and happy. I do everything I can (for the most part) to make it all easier for you including picking up all the things you like to eat.

I get burnt out and I am scared some days too.

Love u lots

Talk to u later today.

Cynda

From: Michael
To: Cynda
Date: Friday, April 25, 2008 11:32 AM
Subject: maybe we can hit the casino

Dont forget BF loves you every minute of the day. It might get harder to show as energy levels seem very demanding but metally [mentally] its there. Don't have to worry or forget its not on. Fiancee's don't need to worry like that.
Will work on chicken
LOVE YOU BF xxxooxxxoxoxo

May 3, 2008

Tonight we had dinner with three golfing couples at Green Basil Thai Cuisine in Burnaby.

May 5, 2008

We had a nice Mother's Day brunch for Mae, Michael's mom at Horizons Restaurant. My eldest son Andrew was working that day and was our server.

> *From: Michael*
> *To: Cynda*
> *Date: Tuesday, May 6, 2008 3:07 PM*
> *Subject: nice to hear you today*
>
> *Hi Honey pOT PIE,*
> *IT was so nice to hear your call this morning. There were a few I think, [phone calls] I can't put together when dad called and baree.*
>
> *oh well, i never quite get enough sleep thru. and yet i probably only need another hour max. but... others have their needs.*
>
> *got enough energy to make dinner. you just have to make broccoli. and some rice okay.*
>
> *so low cook till six*
>
> *very, very,very, very special lamb shanky dinner for glamour pussy and friends. Sorry Ricardo [a chef on Food Network] not welcome here.*
>
> *BF xxxxxxoooxx*
>
> *From: Cynda*
> *To: Michael*
> *Date: Tuesday, May 6, 2008 4:06 PM*
> *Re: nice to hear you today*
>
> *Hi dear,*
>
> *Good talking to u too.*

Leaving now. Will make broccoli and ricy.

From: Michael
To: Cynda
Date: Thursday, May 8, 2008 10:19 AM
Subject: new, fresh mail, kinda like flet

Hi honey, Im going back to nap a bit. Tired 1 hr after waking.No breakfast yet, But energy level is rising a bit. Kevin woke me at 9. to give me his dates. He is so impatient and hyper. It makes me jitter.
I can hardly wait for you come home and calm everything down; call me soon. i guess. i forgot about gas guy, [delivery person from Medigas] last wk he was here between `1230 and 1. after I called him on cell he appeared instantly.

LoveBF xxxxoooxxx

Michael had taken up a new tender gesture of leaving me love notes posted to the mirror in the bathroom. Just little snippets about how he was feeling. I treasure those now. He constantly amazed me at his thoughtfulness. His health was deteriorating, yet he often remained positive. He was dealing with so many health issues, swelling in his feet, skin hurting, bloating and constipation. His courage continued to astound me and I had so much admiration for him.

I remember so many tender moments with Michael. When Michael was healthier, we showered together almost daily. Nearer the end it took so much energy for him to get in and out of the shower. Then I helped him to bathe and dry off. He had a tough time with washing his hair as the sensation of water running over his

head made him feel like he was suffocating. He would
get around this by washing his hair with a washcloth.

I missed the tenderness and the love but it couldn't
be helped. When we did shower together Michael would
lovingly wash my hair.

**There was such tenderness that I savour the feel of it to this day. He
always took such good care of me, much more than I may have realized
at that particular moment. Fortunately, I did realize just how much he
loved me while he was alive.**

Some weekends though, he drove me round the bend.
He couldn't help how he felt, and often a sense of
urgency was in the forefront. Get in as much living
while the living was good. He did know how to relax
but when he had a plan (always have a plan), he would
write out what we needed to do. He'd have his list in
hand and off we would go to run the errands. I now
treasure all those lists that Michael made, as I happened to save some. He would decide what to cook, list
the ingredients that we needed, and then buy what we
did not have.

We always ran errands together. Once he was going to
be making a gourmet dinner for a golfing couple, Sam
and Lana. We went to the dollar store and bought sets
of white dishes so that dinner would be perfect. I
brought over napkins and placemats from my house along
with crystal wine glasses. Michael made a pea soup,
risotto and I made tiramisu. It was a dinner that
rivaled any high end restaurant. He didn't like to do
anything half way and always aimed high.

City Fresh Market was located just a block from home
and it was there that we bought our fresh veggies,

fruit and seafood. Michael would always check in with the same Asian fish guy and get us the best possible. We ate a lot of prawns, black cod, and halibut.

May 11, 2008

Dinner with my family at Mr. Ho's Wonton House, a restaurant in Burnaby for my mom's Mother's Day.

> *From: Michael*
> *To: Cynda*
> *Date: Tuesday, May 13, 2008 11:16 AM*
> *Subject: dinner*
>
> *Hi Sweetee,*
> *Still havn't decided on dinner yet. Maybe Spot prawns, if they're freshies. Do we need vegies but we are definitely having soup. Neckbones already brewing for soup now. I'll put some carrots in there for now and find some sort of leeks or qua [melon] to put in.*
>
> *I miss you, can't wait for u ,,, please respond special agent cynda*
>
> *Lvoe Bjg F;et (special code version)*
>
> *From: Cynda*
> *To: Michael*
> *Date: Tuesday, May 13, 2008 2:04 PM*
> *Subject: RE: dinner*
>
> *Hi Honey aka BF*
> *I can pick up some chinese vegs. Will talk to u when I get off the bus.*
> *I did pick up spicy spareribs though from a special rest.*
> *Love u lots*
> *Cynda*

From: Michael
To: Cynda
Date: Tuesday, May 13, 2008 2:39 PM
Subject: RE: dinner

okay honey,

i got cranrasp juice, choy sum , [Chinese vegetable] a
corn cob, and a moo gua [melon] for our soup. the soup is
brewing happily. still no idea about dinner execpt we got
cheese and could have a quesidilla. what do you think,
YES I'm talkin to you. Yo Dog ... Check it Out.

Love GP's BF American Idol tonite.

["Yo Dog" was a frequent phrase of one of the judges on American Idol.]

May 19, 2008

Because of Michael's family commitments we delayed
celebration of my birthday by a day, and tonight we
had dinner at Sawasdee Thai Restaurant.

May 24, 2008

We went to BC Place for Eat! Vancouver, an annual
foodie event. His family helped to drive us there as
Michael was now often using a wheelchair.

Michael with his favourite chef, Bob Blumer

From: Michael
To: Cynda
Date: Tuesday, May 27, 2008 1:39 PM
Subject: got vacation mail
Hi, Honey pot pie,

I got your email about vacation time. I will look about in a short while. I want to go have a wee nap first, then I'll look for stuff. Had half of the soup. Other half in the pot for now.

See when you get home honey po [pot] pie I love you so much, call anytime.right now if you want.email will be slower for sure. like snail mail , I like email honey po . [honey pot pie]

Love BF xxxxxxoooooxx

As time progressed, the content of Michael's emails began to change. His cognitive ability was failing and it was harder to understand him as he was no longer articulate. As well, spelling, grammar and punctuation were lacking. It is also likely that the medications he was taking had an effect as well.

After much thought, I have decided not to correct the spelling and syntax in Michael's emails. I feel that by doing so, I would be compromising the essence of how he was expressing his thoughts and feelings. Emails already tend to be less structured and will contain abbreviations, typos and lack punctuation.

I have however, added explanations or the correct word or words to the emails in square brackets at the appropriate place. I hope that this helps to clarify what Michael is conveying. In some cases I may not have had an explanation and this is because it is clear enough to figure out his meaning or I do not know what he meant.

> *From: Cynda*
> *To: Michael*
> *Date: Tuesday, May 27, 2008 1:56 PM*
> *Subject: got vacation mail*
>
> *Hi ... aka Big Flet and my honey,*
> *Love you so much you know. I know that you know but I*
> *need to tell you often as well.*
> *In the last few days and weeks, I see more and more of how*
> *things are a struggle for you and I get really scared. I can't*
> *say much more than this or I will start a flood at my desk.*
> *You mean everything to me. I am grateful all the time that*
> *we found each other.*
> *I really need some time away with you. No schedules,*
> *just relaxation. I really also think a change of scenery is*
> *important for you too.*
> *I didn't want to call you as I don't want to wake u. You*
> *really need the rest. I am going to have my cell on in a few*
> *mins.*
> *Going to call in O2 to Medigas as well. I will give them*
> *a heads up that we will need another concentrator and*
> *also gas (5 large and 3 small) for Harrison Hot Springs for*
> *delivery for June 10 or 11 or 12. Two of those days. I will*

tell them that we will confirm this in the next day or so.
We can book our getaway tonite.
Love u

June 3, 2008

I received an email from the social worker.

From: Lily
To: Cynda
Date: Tuesday, June 3, 2008 12:56 PM
Subject: FW: Information

Hi Cynda,

I'm glad we could speak on the phone today. I will speak with Michael's Home Care Nurse, Rainbow, and Occupational Therapist, Iris, this afternoon.

Here is some information that might be helpful to you and Michael.

This is the link to information about the Employment Insurance - Compassionate Care Benefit: http://www. hrsdc.gc.ca/en/ei/types/compassionate_care.shtml

This is our program's brochure -
<<IHPCP brochure.pdf>>

Here are a few links that answer frequently asked questions such as 'what is palliative care?' -
http://www.hospicebc.org/faqs.php
http://www.bccancer.bc.ca/PPI/copingwithcancer/palliative/ default.htm
http://www.chpca.net/menu_items/faqs.htm#faq_whatis

Take good care,
Lily

June 4, 2008

Michael's mom ordered a full face oxygen mask for him from Medigas as it would enable him to inhale more oxygen.

From: Lily
To: Cynda
Date: Thursday, June 5, 2008 9:31 AM
Subject: RE: Information

Glad to hear a few things are falling into place. Please let me know whenever you feel I could provide some support, information, etc.

Lily

From: Cynda
To: Lily
Date: Thursday, June 5, 2008 4:11 PM
Subject: RE: Information

Thank you Lily, it is all becoming very overwhelming at times now as Michael has been deteriorating. I just want him to be as comfortable as possible.
Rainbow was most helpful yesterday in providing me with a great deal of information.

Entry in journal Michael gave to me June, 2008

June 2008

Picked up this beautiful journal for my sweetee at "Gayatri Treasures" in Steveston, BC. The artwork on the book is just wonderful. I am certain you will enjoy this for a long long time.

For Michael, Love Cynda

I got this book for you to enter anything you want from songs, books, titles to recipes. - anything you love.

A book like this comes very easy to give to someone I am continually in love with. I hope there will be countless tales and events in here for years to come.

It never ceases for me to believe how you adapt to the changing conditions that I encounter day to day.

Absolutely nobody does it like you. It just always reminds me that you are truly my Soul mate.

I love you Honey!

With love from Michael & Spidyr

June 6, 2008

The occupational therapist emailed me and let me know that she had contacted Michael.

She said she would be more than happy to order any equipment that Michael needs through the Red Cross Palliative Program; although this program does have some limitations in what they offer.

She had offered a hospital bed and cane and he declined both. He did agree to a bath and tub seat which she has just ordered. She advised that she has added a four wheeled walker to the list upon speaking to his nurse so that he is better able to walk and transport his oxygen tank.

As Rainbow the nurse mentioned that his bed and couch are now becoming difficult to get off of, she suggested bed blocks which could be purchased from Linens 'n Things on Bridgeport Road. She explained that these

little four inch risers can be placed under the legs
of the couch or bed and come in packs of four for
about $15.99.

She also added that she had a foam wedge which Michael
can have as a sleeping aid.

She said she would be more than happy to meet with us
at home to review his needs and would try to arrange
to visit along with the nurse.

With regards to Home Care Physical Therapy she said
she can certainly ask for one of the therapists to
see Michael. She explained that the physio assessment usually consists of providing recommendations
for reducing the risk of falls, and they may be able
to provide some pain management strategies. She said
to let her know if we wanted her to make the referral
to the Physiotherapist and she would do so.

June 11, 2008

Michael had been feeling quite confined to the apartment for some time now. The need for continuous oxygen
limited his options, as well as the need to use the
wheelchair. We had been looking into possible vacations for a few weeks now. Going on a cruise, Harrison
Hot Springs or returning to our precious Anacortes.

Baree and Molly had agreed to drive us to Anacortes
for a day trip but we never did go. I don't recall
why, but it might have been concern with travelling to
the United States with Michael's state of health.

In the end we decided on Harrison Hot Springs and
would go up on a Wednesday and return on the Friday.
It was our last vacation before Michael died. Dick,

Baree and Eric drove us to and from Harrison Hot Springs. It was a lot of coordinating to make this trip happen. As oxygen was delivered weekly to the apartment, I found out that Medigas could also deliver the oxygen and pick up the used tanks from Harrison Hot Springs. Everything was ready and we would be able to go.

I booked much needed massages for both of us. Our time at Harrison was spent going for walks, having leisurely and relaxing meals, napping and using the hot springs. It did us both a world of good and the change of scenery made a big difference.

June 15, 2008

I sent this email to various therapists and support professionals that we had been dealing with.

I am sending you this email from Michael's address on his behalf. My name is Cynda Yeasting and I am Michael's partner.

We have some concerns about his oxygen usage. Since this past Friday he has gone through 4 E, 5 D and 3 C. This is in conjunction with some usage outside the home. He does of course use the concentrator for much of the time in the house.

The O2 is mostly being used in the middle of the night as he feels more secure with them. The O2 is continous and that is what he is missing with the concentrator. He has anxiety when trying to sleep.

Can you please contact him on Monday around 11:00 am to help with this? Ideally if you could come to see him that might help more.

*He is also unable to find a comfortable resting position
wherein he feels he is getting enough O2. Is this something that you can assist him with as well? If not he has an
OT, Iris Shapiro. I am copying her on this email as well.*

*He is often tired and cannot rest for long enough periods
of time due to position as well as air intake. (Note to
Iris, the wedge is no longer helping Michael to sleep.
Can you assist with perhaps a smaller one or something
else? Thanks.)*

CHAPTER ELEVEN
LOVE NEARLY CONQUERS ALL

June 21 and 22, 2008

Parts of the weekend had been much too busy but other parts were lazy and relaxing. On Saturday we slept in which was a real treat. That evening we went to our favourite Japanese restaurant, Sushi Hachi with family for dinner. It was so much tougher for him now as he had less energy and complete reliance on oxygen. We dined on chirashi, daikon, ikura (for Michael of course), spicy scallop roll and negitoro roll. After dinner we went back to the apartment for a dessert of fresh Richmond strawberries, sponge cake, french vanilla frozen yogurt and whipped cream.

We had Sunday dinner with Michael's parents, children and my son, Jeremy. Jeremy came out by bus in the late afternoon. He and I picked up fruit and veggies from the local farm market.

> *From: Cynda*
> *To: Michael*
> *Date: Monday, June 23, 2008 7:59 AM*
> *Subject: Morning*
>
> *Hi Honey*
> *Please let me know by phone if you are okay if I call Dr.*

Khatib (if you don't do it.) I want him to see you to try to resolve (if possible) the issue of your gasping. It isn't going to go away and I expect it will only get worse. I am worried and scared of you having real distress in the middle of the night.

If the dryer guy calls or landlady calls, arrange it for tomorrow or Wednesday. Everything doesn't have to be done today.

Reminder that the OT, I actually think it is a physio that is coming to help you with SLEEP, POSTURE, and BREATHING. I am planning to be at lunch from 12:30 to 2:00 pm but could take some time, to talk to her when she gets there if you want.

Also I will email the RT, Linda about your air usage.

From: Cynda
To: Linda
Date: Monday, June 23, 2008 8:02 AM
Subject: FW: Michael Chu – Oxygen Usage

I have not heard back from you, nor has Michael. We ordered 12 tanks from medigas last week, they were delivered on Thursday. He has gone through 7 e as well as 3 d since then and I am concerned that he will run out before this week's delivery. He has only 2 d and 2 c.

Tks

June 23, 2008

I came home from work feeling pretty exhausted. It had been a rough night with Michael, oxygen, breathing and comfort issues. I probably only got four hours of sleep and I really felt it. I was feeling more and more tired, lack of sleep and too much worry and just the day in and day out of looking after Michael.

I napped a bit on the bus and came home shortly after 5 pm. I was totally pooped. Saw my dear was snoozing comfortably on the wedge and two pillows on the bed. His belly was rising and falling with each subsequent breath.

I came to lay down with him and have a rest. I know of late, sleep is preferred to eating. Once I was anxious to get dinner. Now resting, sleeping and just lying down together is so much more important.

Dinner - what to eat, it was our daily dilemma. So many factors, was Michael hungry, what was he craving, could his stomach handle it, etc.

Still no regrets though, and for that I am very grateful as it reinforces to me that I never doubted my choice of meeting and falling for Michael. Loving him was inevitable for me and has given me some of the greatest gifts in my life. I told him just a few days ago and I am pretty sure I have told him this before that because of him, he has taught me how to love again and how to trust again. I had lost the ability for both for so many years. I was just walking around beaten and downtrodden from about 1992 to 2003. It was much too long a period of time to just exist and not live. It wasn't until I had the hysterectomy in 2003 that I turned my life around. I had already made some mini steps towards changing my life by selling my condo and changing jobs.

We woke up around 7ish. I had mentioned that for lunch, I had a donair. He said he was tired of the usual Chinese food and really needed a different taste. Donair really appealed to him. There was nothing out in Richmond and the mall was already long closed for the evening.

We decided to go to the place close to Granville and 70th. I was concerned about Michael's driving ability as he seemed so tired and dozy. He reassured me that he was just relaxed and fine.

Michael got emotional at the donair place, eyes welling up and telling me how lucky we are. I gently teased him for getting all emotional as that was usually my thing.

As we were low on fuel, I learned to pump gas for the first time. We usually bought gas in Richmond where all the gas stations were full service.

After leaving the donair place Michael drove in a different direction. At first I thought we were going to go to see his Aunt Shirley and Uncle Tim. Instead we headed towards Langview Golf Course.

When he was a kid he remembered hitting the ball against the shack that was there. He also showed me the airport which you could see across the Fraser River. Michael wanted some of his remains to be sprinkled here.

Nowadays it was unusual for Michael to be driving this far from home. He hasn't been driving much and only for short distances as it was too physically tiring. It was a warm, clear and balmy night. The sun still shone brightly and we soaked up the warmth. A few golfers were on the course.

He drove through the parking lot, back to the main road and then down the back alley just behind the 13th hole. The 13th hole was Michael's favourite and we had come here on December 8th. He told me that he did not want to propose to me then because he knew I was expecting him to do so.

He was the guy who never wanted anyone to figure him out. He was so much like me it is scary. I always like to be one step ahead and never want anyone to figure out who I am. It may be a defense mechanism. Anyways Michael knew me better than I knew myself and I like to think that I knew him the same way.

He parked the car and we got out to walk over to the 13th hole. I lamented out loud that I didn't have my camera and wished that I did.

He put his arms around me and asked "Will You Marry Me?" I burst into tears and couldn't stop crying. Of course I said yes. It was perfect. He had always known that this was important to me, to be asked and asked properly. Having Michael finally utter these very special four words made the circle complete. I had always told him I didn't need to have a fancy dinner setting either. It just had to be special. When he gave me the ring on December 13th it was special.

He has also told me that if it were not for his predicament he would have happily been married to me. We had talked about all of this before as well as the legal aspects and I told him I didn't need to be married. I love him more than I could love anyone else, and he was and would always be more than a husband to me. I also thought of him as my husband and I talked about him to strangers that way. It just always felt right.

CHAPTER TWELVE
END OF THE LINE

June 24, 2008

This day turned out to be one of the toughest in our lives. Last night Michael asked me to stay with him today and he asked me again that morning. He had an appointment with the oncologist Dr. Verdana that afternoon for 1:15 pm and I told him that I would meet him there on my lunch hour. At one point he said don't worry about it and don't come. He then waffled and said that I should take the afternoon off and work next week to make up the time during my holiday day, on July 2nd when I had a few routine medical appointments of my own scheduled. I told him I didn't want to do that and I would see what I could do about not returning to the office afterwards. I said I would have taken the afternoon off if I had given work a heads up earlier.

In the end I called work and told the HR person about Michael, his cancer and apologised. As expected it wasn`t a problem and she was most understanding.

Dick picked us up as usual to go to the BC Cancer Agency Clinic. I went with Michael to the lab for blood tests first and then to the x-ray. He still had his sense of humor and said that he was there for his photo session.

We had an hour or more before the appointment with Dr. Verdana and went to the cafeteria where Michael had a yogurt and half a banana. He wanted to have something healthy and clean to eat. I wanted to go to Ichibankan Express to pick up some chicken curry and wakame seaweed salad and left Michael to do that.

When I returned, we went to the 2nd floor to check in for our appointment with Dr. Verdana. We also needed to find out where we could get hooked up to oxygen, so as not to deplete our supply.

We soon knew that the news would not be good as Dr. Verdana, who is always late, was early. There was a mix up about the appointment time and we were about one hour early and even so, Dr. Verdana was still about half an hour early.

I really think in our hearts, we have known for weeks that the news was not going to be good. Six weeks ago when they were still willing to continue Michael on the Tarceva, I was surprised and relieved. I didn't expect him to get more medication as he was still deteriorating and had been for some time now, weeks at least. I had already spoken to family members about seeing Michael more frequently and everyone was coming through.

Dr. Verdana was sombre and told us that the cancer is spreading and that to treat Michael further would be malpractice. Michael asked him what that meant. Dr. Verdana explained that he is so frail now that it would do more harm than good to try to treat him. He said that the test results six weeks ago had already indicated that the drug was no longer working but they had decided to give it the benefit of the doubt and continue one more course. He added that Michael may feel better after stopping the Tarceva as the drug causes inflammation of the lungs and that the inflammation would decrease after stopping.

He reiterated this and said again that there are no further treatment options, no trials available as well, as nothing anywhere else would work or help. Michael had such a brave face and he forced himself to be composed. I know I cried afterwards, I don't remember if Michael did or not.

The doctor also said I am sorry Mr. Chu (or perhaps it was Sir, I cannot remember now) but you are now effectively dying from the cancer.

I cried and talked briefly to Dr. Verdana's nurse at the BC Cancer Agency Clinic. I had gone to look for her and had to go back to the room when Michael called out for me.

Dr. Verdana also said that Michael was too fragile to be driving. It took so much energy for him to get in and out of the car. Just getting into the driver's seat was tough.

Michael resented having that last bit of freedom taken away from him and it confirmed to him that he was getting worse. He really enjoyed driving and he had lost that right for a brief time earlier. It happened when he was first getting treatment and blacked out.

Now instead of driving in the neighborhood, I would set him up in the wheelchair and off we would go. I would always bring an extra cylinder of oxygen as well as additional tubing.

I am the type of person that likes to be prepared and so I always did my best to ensure that we had everything we needed before heading out. Michael needed constant oxygen and I couldn't risk running out when we were not at home. I would also bring additional Morphine. One time when we were out, the tubing got caught in Michael's wheelchair, tore and I had to immediately replace the tubing.

Nearer the end when we went out, I would also pack the Ventilator which Michael fondly called the Bombadier. Another Michaelism. He called Basmati rice, spasmodic rice; landed immigrants were landed ignorants. Although it was a conscious choice to live in Richmond, he was frustrated with the Asian drivers as well as the traffic jams on No. 3 Road which he called Ho Chi Minh Trail.

We then went up to the 6th floor where they administer chemotherapy treatments. Michael wanted to say hello to Elizabeth, a nurse who had seen him through many chemo treatments but unfortunately she was at lunch. It felt like this would be the last time that Michael would ever come here. I hope not, but it felt that way. We have another appointment with Dr. Verdana on August 19. It was a quiet ride home.

We told Dick what Dr. Verdana told said when we got to the car. He didn't really have any response and I wasn't sure if he was in shock but it was like he couldn't absorb what we had told him. Neither could we, it was all too much.

We arrived at his parents and picked up Michael's car and we went to the A & W Restaurant in Richmond.

We would be emotionally eating today; burgers and onion rings. Michael had used the phrase "end of the line" many times as we had thought we were there in the past. There had been many reprieves but today it was reality.

I didn't go back to work after that. I called the office and talked the HR person. I told her that Michael had cancer and it was terminal. This was the first time I had told anyone at work. I had never said anything to anyone as it was self-preservation. I asked if it would be okay for me to be on vacation immediately as I was due to be on vacation the following week. I said I would contact them on the Friday to let them know what was happening.

I was still using the HRT (hormone replacement therapy). I was hesitant to discontinue their use previously as I was concerned about becoming too emotional, but after today's news I am going to lose it and cry anyways, so this was a good a time as any to discontinue them.

June 27, 2008

Today I sent out the following email to all of the family members involved in Michael's care.

> *Because everyone is going to be helping out with Michael's care, I needed to list everything as he isn't able to remember everything as well as he used to and can and does get mixed up. It would also be irresponsible if I am the only one that knows everything.*
>
> *To keep track, I created a medication record. We fill one out daily. We always mark in the time when he takes his medications as well as filling in the amount and times he*

takes the 10 IR. Also he fills in the blood test results and how much insulin he takes.

Morphine and Dex - take between 6 to 8 am, between 2 to 4 pm and 10 to 11 pm

Morphine comes in a 30 mg pink capsule and he takes 2. Dex comes in three tablets. Two are .5 mg and 1 (the smaller pill) is 2 mg for a total of 3 mg. I give this to him on my work days before I leave.

The times are not set in stone but we want him to have the three doses spread out as evenly as possible. They can make him drowsy. He is also very sleepy each time the dosage is increased by the doctor. He will have dizziness, extreme sleepiness, be unsteady on his feet and be confused. The risk of falling is much greater. This generally lasts from 2 to 3 days from the first day he has the change in medications.

Morphine 10 IR

The tablets are white and 10 mg each. There is a bottle on the dining room table, as well as one by the bed. We each carry a supply for going out. There are a few 5 mg ones left in a bottle on the dining room table as well.

Michael takes these 2 at a time. He takes them when he is feeling gaspy. Give him continuous air from the tank first. The regulator has a black button that can be turned from "conserve" (air intake upon each breath) to "continous" (constant air flow).

If after taking the 2 10 mg IR, he does not feel relief within a minute or two, give him the option of taking a third tablet. He might need Ativan (kept by the bedside by the bear) as he is anxious and cannot relax. One tablet under the tongue. This works immediately and water might be needed to dissolve it.

All his medicines except for the 10 IR (which is the instant release Morphine that he takes on an as needed basis) are sorted out by Breakfast, Lunch, Supper and Bedtime in little blue plastic boxes for each day of the week. I make up a new set for the week each Sunday.

There are also some holistic medications that he takes on a daily basis and are in the blue boxes. They are 1 Vitamin D, 2 Mushroom, 1 Ginseng and 1 Royal Jelly.

He also takes Advil gel caps and Sennoket on an as needed basis. Sennoket is for bowel movement as the Morphine makes him constipated.

For his oxygen use he has a gel as well as a nose spray. These he uses as the oxygen dries out his nasal passages.

The blue boxes are kept on the dining room table and generally so is the Advil and Sennoket.

Contact people:

All their business cards have been scotch-taped to the office wall by the calendar. There are some I couldn't find. As well there are others that are not listed here as they are not as relevant; the Diabetes doctor and denturist for example.

Dr. Clark Khatib - Palliative doctor

Office is 778-276-5555. Cell is 778-240-5555. Both these numbers should be in both phones. Listed under "Dr." He makes house calls. He is really good about coming to see

Michael the same or next day. Getting an appointment for the same day generally works out.

He has two nurses, Ellen and Mary. They are on a work share. He works (as far as we know.) Mondays through Saturdays and also works out of Richmond Hospital where the palliative care unit is located.

When calling the office you can leave a VM message for him. I don't call his cell unless it is of some urgency. Michael is having trouble breathing and the dosage needs to be changed, etc. Also when you call the office after hours, there is always a doctor on call and his cell # is left as well as his name. He always returns calls.

Various Professionals under Vancouver Coastal Health 604-278-3361

Rainbow Chan - Home Care Nurse

She comes to check in on Michael. She calls either weekly or comes in whenever Michael wants to see her. She is always very good about call backs when you leave her a message.

She can be reached at the general number or by email at Rainbow.Chan@vch.ca

Iris Shapiro and Viola Kam - Occupational Therapists

Iris can be reached at ext. 5588 and by email at iris.shapiro@vch.ca

Viola can be reached the general number or by email at viola.kam@vch.ca

Linda Huynh - Respiratory Therapist

She is the one that measures the amount of oxygen that Michael is getting and comes periodically to measure it. We are currently awaiting recent monitoring to see if his levels are still the same at night or not.

She can be reached at the general number or by email at linda.huynh@vch.ca.

Lily Jackson - Clinical Social Worker
Integrated Hospice Palliative Care Program
Richmond Health Services
phone (604) 555-9711 local 5555

She is the resource person for any information required. She sent me the following when I had asked for it.

Here are a few links that answer frequently asked questions such as "what is palliative care?" -
http://www.hospicebc.org/faqs.php
http://www.bccancer.bc.ca/PPI/copingwithcancer/palliative/default.htm
http://www.chpca.net/menu_items/faqs.htm#faq_whatis

Oxygen and Humidifier -

Oxygen is currently provided by Medigas (604-527-0744) but this is going to be changing over the course of the next few months. Government has contracted two other companies. VitalAire and MedPro Respiratory Care (MedPro). Everything will stay the same. They will contact Michael. Once the new company is set up then Medigas will pick up old equipment. We have no choice in this matter as his oxygen is being paid for by the government.

Currently the order is placed each Tuesday (during the business day) and then delivered each Thursday (usually by 1:30 pm). Cynda calls in the order. Also asks for any necessary tubing or bags for tanks. We are getting 12 tanks per week and we get to choose the size. Currently ordering 10 E and 2 D.

All the tanks are kept in the dining room with the empties in the back row. I also leave a large new tank in the bedroom all the time. We only have one regulator and that is on the tank that he is currently using. It is either attached to one in the bedroom or the portable one for going out.

I used to keep two tanks in the car but no longer do this as the car is rarely used anymore.

He uses the concentrator, located in the office. This runs continuously when we are at home. Parents have one at their house as well. There is an air filter on it that needs to be washed weekly. When we are out we use the portable tanks and always take an extra tank and sometimes two. These extras are in addition to the one that the regulator is hooked up to. The concentrator is turned off just before we leave and back on as soon as we come back home.

To give Michael more air, an air conditioner is turned on in the bedroom. The window and door has to be closed when it is on. Just press the button on the bottom far left. The fan is generally left on to keep the air moving.

We also keep the living room balcony door open as well as the dining room fan on and the light off.

Please remember no lotions, soaps, hand creams, perfumes or scents of any kind as it constricts Michael's breathing passages. It might not be a strong smell to you but it bothers Michael.

We also have to close the balcony door when the neighbor smokes outside.

The cool mist humidifier is turned on throughout the night to keep the air moist. I refill it with water every night.

Water, drinking -

Always take water with us when we go out in case Michael needs to take medication in the car or while out in the wheelchair. Also water is always kept on the table next to Michael when he is sleeping in case he needs it.

Pharmacy -
All prescriptions are filled at the London Drugs at 5971 No. 3 Road, Richmond, BC 604-278-4521

They also have a service wherein they deliver the pre-scriptions in the evening to us.

Dr. Marshall Verdana - Oncologist

He is at the BC Cancer Agency Clinic and can be reached at the general number of 604-877-6000.

Lori Wellman - Nurse

She is at the BC Cancer Agency Clinic and can be reached at 604-877-6098, local 5555 or by email at lstacey@bccancer.bc.ca. She works with Dr. Verdana and can be contacted to answer any questions.

Adam Young - Counsellor

He can be reached at the BC Cancer Agency Clinic at 604-877-6000, local 5555.

For Michael, Love Cynda

PENDING

Hospital bed is being delivered this Wed, July 2nd between 1:00 pm to 4:00 pm by the Red Cross.

Home care of 4 hours per day is being arranged and we will finalize how we want to use this with Rainbow on Monday. If friends and family members can be here the other times when I am at work, this will keep Michael covered.

When I look at this list now, it is daunting and over-whelming, I honestly don't know how we managed to deal with so many people.

June 29, 2008

Michael had been wanting to go see the new Adam Sandler movie, Don't Mess with the Zohan and so we were going tonight with Baree and Molly after dinner.

At dinner we had a disagreement and I left the table to go to the ladies' room. During that time Michael told Baree and Molly that he feels like he has become an old man and he can no longer do anything anymore. Everyone was still who they were, but he had become very old overnight.

It broke my heart a little more to hear this. I had been struggling a great deal with my own feelings for a number of months now. I saw Michael every day and I saw his deterioration up front.

Michael had wanted to see the movie so badly but wasn't able to stay awake for much of it. We were all concerned that he was so tired.

June 30, 2008

Dr. Khatib provided a letter for me so that I could receive Compassionate Care benefits through EI. These benefits are provided to persons who have to be away from work temporarily to provide care or support to a family member who is gravely ill with a significant risk of death. In it he stated that Michael had metastatic lung cancer and that his life expectancy was less than six months. It was tough to see this in print.

CHAPTER THIRTEEN
PALLIATIVE CARE

July 1, 2008

Michael woke up very disoriented and weak. He was unable to hold himself up and kept slipping off the bed even though he was sitting up. I could barely hold him up and he was in a semi-conscious state. I was really scared and called his family to come right away. I contacted Dr. Khatib as well. We watched him all day as he slept and during the brief periods when he was awake he was incoherent. Everyone was frightened and there was a lot of tears.

Later that night he woke up and was lucid and talked to all of us. We thought he was going to die that day and he said he thought that as well.

The next day I arranged to have him taken by ambulance to the palliative care unit of the local Hospital. I moved into the hospital with him and we stayed there for just over a week. While he was there they were able to stabilize him. His oxygen levels and medications were adjusted. The change in his health from July 1st was startling. He was eating again as he was hungry and I couldn't be happier to get up in the middle of the night to go warm up something for him.

Staying in the palliative care unit of the hospital was brutal. You were surrounded by many people who were dying of cancer, the pained expressions on their family members' faces showed the immense toll this horrific disease was taking on them. One cancer patient was in such pain you often heard her moaning. The cancer had spread to her soft organs and no amount of pain medication was enough to bring her any relief.

This same day, I sent the following email to my siblings:

Michael has been deteriorating more and more in the last several weeks.

We were at the BC Cancer Agency Clinic this past Tuesday and the oncologist has taken him off all cancer treatment drugs now. There is nothing more that they can do for him as the cancer is spreading and he is too frail to take anything more, nor is there anything that will work. I have not returned to work since.

His condition really started to go downhill around June 19th and got worse starting on June 23rd.

He sleeps much of the time and doesn't seem to be in any pain. He is often confused and sometimes paranoid. Dr. says it could be the meds or an underlying problem. (The cancer could be back in his brain.)

The man who was so crazy about eating now has dif- ficulty getting a few bites of food down. He has almost no appetite and it is tough to get him to eat.

He has taught me to be braver than I ever thought I could be. He has also given me such love and caring that I have never had before. For all of this and so many other reasons I am very grateful.

I love you guys very much.

Cynda

Michael and Spyder taking a nap

July 10, 2008

Michael was well enough to go back home after our grueling but successful hospital stay. He was doing better now than he has in the past six weeks to two months. His appetite is back to normal and he is breathing well. He has some anxiety but I think it will ease off as he is settled back home.

I never thought leaving palliative care to return home was ever an option. Michael's health turnaround was a small miracle.

His family was naturally concerned about this but I was adamant that if I could manage, I would continue to do so. Having Michael back home would make him happy. There were a lot of adjustments and changes. Our time was filled with consultations with social workers, nurses, respiratory therapists and doctors.

July 15, 2008

Although the hospital bed was originally scheduled to be delivered July 2nd, I cancelled it as Michael checked into palliative care that day. It was provided by the Red Cross and was placed next to the regular bed. Michael didn't want to use it as it would be admitting that he was that sick.

As Michael had an appetite again, we were busy for the next couple of weeks with lunches and dinners and catching up with friends.

July 19, 2008

I sent the following email to all of Michael's family members:

> *As you all know Michael has been extremely sleepy since this past Tuesday. We thought perhaps that part of it was the hospital bed or the medication, in particular the Morphine.*
>
> *He has still been eating pretty well but is having more trouble with going to the bathroom.*
> *He slept in the regular bed last night and he did have a better sleep although he has been sleeping much of today. He hasn't been awake for more than 45 mins total. He had 1/2 a grapefruit for breakfast and told me that he is allergic to it. He remembered that he wasn't able to have any grapefruit for the past 10 months while he was on the Tarceva (the cancer pill that he took daily since September*

2007 and which ended on June 24th.) He did eat it and really enjoyed it.

He had a sticky rice made by Janie (a friend of his parents) and really enjoyed that. He drank but not much, only what I could get into him. A bit of tea, (sorry Mae, not even a full cup, even with repeated reminders) and some water.

His palliative doctor, Dr. Khatib was just by and visited for about 20 mins.

He says that Michael's sleepiness is due in part 75% because of the cancer and 25% is due to medications.

Medication changes
He has asked us to increase his steroid dose which is currently at 4 mg to 8 mg for Sunday, Monday and Tuesday. The purpose of doing this is to increase his breathing comfort and it may make him more awake.
He also said to cease taking the morning dose of Clonazepam and cut the evening dose to 1/2 a tablet. This medication makes him drowsy and relaxes him and works similarly to Ativan but is a long term drug.
He has written a new prescription for an amphetamine called Dexadrine. (I think it is a diet pill?). This will give Michael the energy boost. Says that he is to start taking this tomorrow with one at breakfast (doesn't have to be with food but is for timing) and do that for three days. If it does not help enough, then up it to 2 x at breakfast. He says that we can also add one pill at lunch as well but not to take it any later than that otherwise Michael will not sleep.

I am to call him on Wednesday with a report as to whether all of this has helped or not.

Morphine
Says that this is the first thing Michael should take if he is short of breath. It takes 10 to 20 mins to work. Says that if he is due for meds at 2:00 pm, and is short of breath at 1:45 pm, to give him the 3 ml (in between dose) and then the regular dose at 2:00 pm.

I told him that I had been giving Michael his medications according to how I saw the nurses doing it in the hospital. He said that was not correct.

Ventolin
Says that I can give him this at the same time as the Morphine when he is short of breath. I told Dr. that we had been doing with higher air flow and Ventolin before using extra Morphine as Michael and I are concerned about over taking of the medication. He says that it is not a worry and to take it when needed.

Anyways we will need to go to London Drugs to get the prescription filled as well as pick up more Ventolin as the doctor is also calling that in (I forgot to ask him while he was here.)
Choking
Michael has had a few choking episodes of late. Dr. says his throat is fine and lungs sound okay.

July 20, 2008

We had dinner with Michael's parents and family members at their golf country club. Michael was dealing with a lot of mixed emotions. There was some sort of disagreement with a family member at dinner and he became quite upset.

CHAPTER FOURTEEN
HOSPICE CARE

July 27, 2008

Alexandra left on a trip to Europe and we saw her off at the airport. When I look at the pictures now, I see the anguish in her face. Michael really wanted her to take the trip and was adamant that she should go.

It wasn't long before things got more difficult and I had to talk to Michael about going into a hospice. I had strongly resisted doing this as I worried that once he was in one, he wouldn't be with us very long. I could no longer cope with all the responsibilities and the daily care Michael needed. I needed professional help.

Moving into the Salvation Army Rotary Hospice House was admitting that the end was near and that Michael would die there. His health continued to deteriorate and it changed greatly within a week. He was only at the hospice for 12 days before he died.

Michael's room had doors that opened onto a grassy area. A short time after we moved into the hospice, Kailey kindly brought two huge pots of flowers, a table and sundeck chairs so that we had a relaxing outside area to sit in.

While he was in the hospice we still went out; a dim sum lunch given by members of his dad's side of the family on August 3rd and then a family dinner that evening at Koon Bo Restaurant.

August 7, 2008

We had dinner at West, just three days before Michael died. Michael ordered the foie gras starter, spot prawn risotto and grilled squab for his entree. He amazed all of us that he had such an appetite and enjoyed his food right until the very end.

After dinner, back at the hospice, and shortly before midnight Michael typed and sent an email to his daughter Alexandra sharing his dining experience and how he was feeling.

Cynda and Michael at West

On August 8, 2008 I wrote an email to Margy. Here is the majority of it:

> *A week ago this past Sunday I told him that we need to look at going to a hospice. We talked when he left the hospital that we would try it at home as he really wanted to die at home but that if it didn't work there then the hospice was plan b. We were lucky to get in within a couple of days. We toured the facility on Tuesday and then checked in on Wednesday. I also told him that the family was not happy about him going back home, that they were concerned. He never knew that. I think only his son was on his side.*

> *Because of the very short time we had to make all the arrangements, last week went by in a blur as there was so much to do and I was just exhausted. Things were just starting to calm down on Monday. I also started to get more than 2 hours of sleep at a time. It has been some 6 weeks or more that I had decent sleep.*

> *Being at the hospice has made life much easier. It has its challenges though as nurses, housekeeping, volunteers are always around. We don't have to worry about cooking, cleaning and most importantly medications.*

> *Needless to say I have not been at work...*

> *Right now I really don't expect him to last much longer as the breathing is becoming more difficult and he is more confused. He is agitated a lot, hypersensitive to sound and light. Dying slowly is awful. It is so tough for those around the person as well as the person himself. I am doing lots of reading on end of life and hospice so that I can understand more of what to expect. I don't want him to suffer but I also don't want to lose him. It really is catch 22.*

Spyder the cat has moved with us as well and he has been a little upset at times as well. The little rotter peed in a bag of mine that had dried fruit in it. I know that he is scared and upset as well.

It is extra hard as his daughter left for a planned vacation in Europe on July 25th. I know he is just hanging on for her return.

We are also trying to empty out Michael's place as well. Last Saturday, I packed up some of my things and moved them back to my house. I was back there yesterday and pretty much packed up all that I needed to get. My house of course is a disaster as I have had no time to unpack or put too much away. His place looks so sad and empty now.

A couple of days ago he said I seem to be tormented and I told him I am. I said that sometimes it might seem like I don't care and it is my way of dealing as each day that I spend with him I am saying goodbye to him more and more.

I keep having anxiety nightmares. Michael is always part of my dreams and I am always trying to reach or find him. I don't want to leave him while he is here but at the same time I know I need little breaks.

I am going to try to get out for an hour or so today as I need to get away a bit. Is that wrong to feel this way? I don't think so and he knows it too but he struggles as well. I love him so much.

He has a friend coming this am and while he is here I am going to unroll my mat and practice yoga. I haven't worked out since late June. No time nor energy or inclination.

He is taking Ventolin through a breathing mask right now. We have all the comforts of home here, tv, dvd player, microwave, coffee maker, fridge, and internet. He has been losing his memory for some time now and his cognitive ability is fading. It is so hard at times seeing how he has changed. He was an extremely smart and witty man. He still has some wit but it is much tougher for him now. I dread the day when he is no longer him.

As for your aunt, I hope that you are able to accompany her so that she can go. I know that you have always been very close to her and it would be a wonderful gift to her and yourself to spend that extra time with her and as you say it may be her last trip.

Life is truly short and I have always been very scared of having to deal with illness like this. I don't know where I got the courage to do this but I don't think I thought about it too much but just did it. Ironically or maybe it was a premonition, I got a tattoo shortly before I met Michael. It is in Chinese and it is the words 'brave' and 'courageous'. I did it to remind myself to continue to be. I try to challenge myself and always strive for more and different experiences no matter how scary it is.

I am glad that you are my friend Margy and I send my love to you. I often wish you were not so far away. I wish you and Marc could have met Michael. He is a very strong person and although we have had some feisty disagreements, he is the love of my life and there will never be another for me like him. I feel very fortunate to have found love like this as I never expected it would happen.

The pain now is well worth the happiness we have had.

Love
Cynda

August 9, 2008

It is raining today and this morning Michael woke up struggling to breathe and was given more breakthrough doses of Morphine. He is very tired and it is a difficult time for all of us. Spyder feels the stress as he pooped and peed on Michael's bed.

His friend Cynthia came to visit us around noon and brought Spyder a red leash. She told Michael how much she loves him. She asked him if he knew where he was before he was born. That made him really think and ponder.

She also told him to hang on. She had no idea how tough things had been for Michael in the last little while. I had told him that I am selfish and don't want him to go but that I didn't want him suffering anymore. Part of his fear I think was the actual dying process. Would it be painful? Would it linger?

After Cynthia left, Michael and I continued their conversation about life and death. Michael wondered why things had turned out the way they did. I asked him if he wondered how it came to be that he was born to his parents and that he was born in Vancouver and not that he was born in say, Ethiopia. I told him all of our lives were planned before we came to be and that God or a greater power had figured out all of our lives. Our meeting was all part of this as well.

Michael rested for a bit, but not well. He had to take more medications and he was so very tired of having to do this as it was constant and never ending. I told him I know he was so tired of doing this.

This morning Michael asked me to call his parents as well as Eric, Baree and Molly. He wanted them to come to the hospice as soon as possible. He also did not want his parents to drive there and made a point of asking someone to pick them up. He somehow knew that his time was very near.

He told me later that evening that I have been such a trooper and that he cannot go on any longer and that I need to have my life back.

Before Michael died, either on the Friday or Saturday, I cannot remember for certain which, he said to me early in the morning "Did I hear about this place? That if he never leaves there, he will never die. He will always be okay if he stays there." It sounded to me that he was talking about heaven and that he was preparing to leave.

As I write this I am surrounded by photos of Michael. One on my jewelry box was a real close up of him in his home office. It was taken shortly after I got my Canon camera so it would have been late June, 2007. The camera was a gift from Michael as he wanted me to have a better one. Even though he no longer had a regular income he was generous and spoiled me. Luckily I had many opportunities to spoil him back.

That picture was so special because it was close up and I feel like I can really see him clearly. I have another one of Michael taken at the hospice early in August of him with Spyder. Spyder is wrapped around his right arm and he is lying on the bed. Not smiling but just looking. It was natural and I am ever so grateful that I took so many pictures.

Because we did not know how much time Michael had, I took a lot of pictures as I wanted to collect memories. It was never a problem as he enjoyed taking pictures and being in them. I made a point of taking lots of pictures at every event. After Michael died I was ever so grateful to have documented all our time together with pictures.

His mom had been fighting a cold and wasn't feeling that well. Michael asked her to please spend the night at the hospice and so she did.

I wasn't sure if I was dreaming or if it was real as I was exhausted and Michael was awake so much between midnight and 3:00 am but one of the times that he laid down I am sure he said night night Sweetee, I love you (When he wished me a good night, he always said "night night"). I am pretty sure that this is the last thing he ever said to me.

CHAPTER FIFTEEN
GOODBYE HONEY

August 10, 2008

Today was one of the saddest days in my life. The love of my life, Michael Kip Chu left this world and now I have to figure out how I am going to live without him. I am in shock so far and thinking that he is okay at home and that I will phone him shortly before I go to bed. But my baby, my darling man is no longer here.

A few days earlier we sat next to each other on the bed and he said "Fuck, I love you so much." A day or so after, he said that he loves me so deeply.

I went to run an errand with Mary Anne this morning and before we left we both told Michael we were going out for a short time.

Before we went out, Michael was given an injection by one of the nurses. We were told that it was to help him as his breathing was getting more difficult. We were also told at that time that Michael was likely to pass away later today or tomorrow. The impression I got was that it was more likely to be tomorrow. In the end I think Michael passed away about an hour after the injection was given.

When we got back to the hospice his dad came out and said to us, he's gone, he just... I ran, hysterically through the hospice to Michael. I flew past the nurse's station and I heard someone say "Is that Cynda?" I got to the room and there was my Michael, looking restful and at peace. I couldn't believe that I wasn`t there when he took his last breath. I felt just sick that I wasn't there for Michael and heaved in the bathroom. I was later told by Molly that her dad sent her home and then he passed away. Also by Rhea, Michael's cousin that her sister Kailey was with their father endlessly and he died as soon as she went to the bathroom.

I never knew how I would be with someone who has died as I have never been there when it happened. It was always much later, at the funeral home that I would see them. This was very different as Michael had been the love of my life. He was the person that I loved most in this world, other than my sons. I couldn't hold or touch him enough. I kept kissing his face, his forehead, his lips and it wasn't scary to me at all. It felt right and then as I held his hands they got colder and colder. I hugged his body close to me. I knew that this was the last time that I would see Michael and I couldn't bear to let him go even though I knew that he was no longer part of this body. The light had already left his body. After seeing him dead, I finally understood the light a person has which is talked about so much in yoga. I never truly understood it before. I told him that he needs to come back to me in my dreams as I need him.

It is 4:00 in the morning now and I woke up and it was cold and no Michael in my dreams. It feels strange and surreal. I feel lost without him.

I spent the morning puttering around the house. I unpacked and sorted things out. Jeremy helped me put some of the things away. I got out just about all the pictures of Michael and I, from the lake, Cuba and at the wedding. It is 1:00 am now and although I should be asleep I find I cannot rest. Thinking about Michael makes me sob uncontrollably.

When Jeremy and his friend went out earlier tonight to pick up dinner, I let out a primal scream and cried. It was a bit of cleansing as I have such pent up pain. Will I ever feel better? Or will it be worse?

Mary Anne called checking up on how I was doing. We spoke about Michael, as well as her life as a kindergarten teacher. I had wanted to be a kindergarten teacher for a number of years but did not pursue it. I feared I would not be able to get into university. I am grateful that she is really a nice person and so easy to like.

August 11, 2008

Molly sent out the following email to everyone to let them know that Michael had died.

> *Hey friends,*
> *Sorry for the mass email but it just works better right now. Michael, Baree's brother passed away yesterday morning. He went peacefully at Richmond hospice while his cousin was with him singing him Beatle songs. The one she was singing to him was "I'll follow the sun" as he passed.*
> *I have attached a few photos from our dinner on Thursday eve when we took Michael for dinner. Baree had given him a certificate for WEST, for him and Cynda for Christmas that he hadn't used it yet. So Baree borrowed his Dad's*

vehicle because it would sit Mike comfortably and accom-
modate his wheel chair and oxygen along with the other
diners.

Michael has always loved to cook and more so in the
past two years and he loooooooved watching the cooking
channel, especially Iron Chef and Hell's Kitchen. He also
wrote reviews at www.dinehere.ca along with Cynda. His
handle was hargow and Cynda's is dawntart.

In the last few months he would invite guests over, have
the ingredients there and then proceed to have everyone
make dinner under his precise direction. Needless to say a
few of us are better chefs for it, especially our Cynda.

So we had quite a bit of fun with him rating the Chef of
West as they do on Iron Chef. He did get a little confused
on the rating system but that probably was to do with this
Morphine cocktail part way thru the dinner. If you can
believe, it he ordered TWO appetizers and a main course.
Of course this was an extremely pricey restaurant. But
to know Michael is to know that he would manage to use
up the whole amount on the certificate for himself. Many
times during the meal he had a pretty big grin on his face
and twice he said WOW when eating his food. I have
never heard Michael say WOW about anything in the 4 1/2
years that I have known him.

Michael managed to continue to enjoy life to the fullest
even though he was unable to golf or fish since last year.
Being with Cynda continued to be his favourite pastime
along with eating fine food whether it was dining in South
Granville or eating at a good Chinese Barbeque (which
was brought in to him Saturday and of course he had to
make his own selection of the meat.)

take care

ciao for now

M

August 13, 2008

His parents put the following obituary notice in the newspaper. They were so considerate that they called me to make sure I was happy with the wording. I was so touched as I could not imagine the anguish they must have been going through.

> "CHU Michael Born March 26, 1954 in Vancouver, BC. Michael passed away on August 10, 2008 at the Richmond Rotary Hospice. He will be missed by his children Alexandra and Eric, parents Mae and Dick, brother Baree, niece Asia and his many aunts, uncles and cousins. A special thanks to his fiance Cynda Yeasting, Maryanne Chu and Molly Spencer for all their loving and compassionate care. Also to his many friends that gave him support during his courageous battle with cancer. No service by request. Donations can be made to the BC Cancer Agency or the Diabetes Foundation."

I wrote the following in the online guest book:

> To my dear honey, Michael aka Flet:
>
> "To the world you may be just one person, but to one person you may be the world" – Brandi Snyder.
>
> You changed my world and I will never be the same again. You gave me gifts that money cannot buy.
>
> You gave me so much love and brought out the best in me and all those that you loved.
>
> I will miss you every day until I can be with you again. I will meet you on the beach in the little hut with the big Palm Tree.

Until then, I will have to cope with all the memories we made. You are in my heart and deep in my soul.

I love you so much.

Love Honey Pot Pie

xoxoxox

Cynda Yeasting
Burnaby, British Columbia

August 18, 2008

The pain is worse. I didn't expect any lessening and it never occurred to me that it would get worse and so much worse. I want to just wail and curl up on the floor and cry. I force myself to do things. Fortunately because I had been away from the house for so very long everything is really dirty. One week later and I still have some of the mess on my living room floor. I feel like I am going crazy. I clean things in a frenzy and I have been doing so at an intensified pace. I bounce from one task to another and sometimes don't complete the original task for hours or that day. I cannot find things. I cannot remember where I put things. I don't want to sleep. I work myself to exhaustion. I think I clean like crazy as I am trying to find some sense of order. To understand why things are the way they are. I always enjoyed baking because you put in the same ingredients and get the same result. Real life doesn't work that way. I loved Michael, more than ever I think, and I know he loves me and that was not enough. I wish he wasn't gone but I didn't want him to suffer. It hurt so much to see him struggle and I just wanted him to be without pain.

The urge to nurture is also extremely strong. I really want plants and to garden. I have never wanted to garden so much in my life. I want plants and flowers and living things around me. I want to cook and bake. I looked at Michael's recipes today and cried. Today I made dinner of flank steak (instead of Michael's two buck Chuck) and ox tail with baby carrots, red potatoes and mushrooms. Jeremy and Jon must have liked it or it could have been the lateness of the dinner hour, around 8 but they went back for seconds so that was good. Jeremy made a comment that it sure is nice to get meals again. I know it was tough for the kids when I wasn't here but now that I am back I wish desperately that I could have it all. I am glad to be back with the kids but the price I had to pay was to lose Michael and that hurts like hell. It is not fair and why is life so difficult? I feel like I cannot breathe and catch myself not exhaling time and time again.

After Michael died, I went to see my family doctor. My test results came back and I am in the clear for at least a week. Doctor wants me to return for further urine test in a week so I will do that.

I have always loved to write and I hope that by writing about Michael it can help to ease some of the pain. I know that it will never go away but will perhaps be softened by fond memories. Michael was my world and although at times it was difficult I couldn't stand not being with him. I am truly exhausted now as it is 2:30 am and I have been going since 9:00 am. I know I must rest and I took an Ativan, .5 mg just now. I don't take them every night but have quite a few times. I need to sleep and I hope that sleep brings me my Michael in my dreams. I need you more than ever now honey.

Saturday, I was going through things in my room and found an empty shoe box containing two post it notes from Michael. I sobbed. I treasure those love notes. Maybe it hurts so much now because I was so very deeply treasured and he is no longer here to love me.

August 19, 2008

It gets worse and it hurts more and more. I can barely breathe at times. I am choked with pain and agony.

I vividly remember all that we have done together. It is like everything I recall is in HD, crystal clear and sharp, Michael would have liked that. Driving to Makaha in the pitch black; stopping at the gas station to buy water; going to Tamura Supermarket to buy ahi tuna, wakame seaweed salad at the deli or pre-cooked ribs that Michael enjoyed.

I remember Cuba like it was yesterday, walking down the hall from our room and showering in the funny bathtub with the smelly toilet water. I remember all the afternoons making love in the king sized bed and then making love in the am and rushing to get to breakfast because we started again. There was so much tenderness and loving. Things were brand new and we savored in the joy of all of it.

After Hawaii, Michael's health really started to deteriorate and our love life was modified with lots of hugs and tenderness. This is probably what I miss the most...the love, the companionship, even though I was the caregiver, Michael always looked after me.

For Michael, Love Cynda

August 24, 2008

Today I thought I was actually okay. What a fool as it has only been two weeks. I just watched portions of Michael's DVD again, the parts in the beginning about his Mom and Dad, Mary Anne and the kids and then myself. I hadn't seen the parts about me again until now and more of what he said registered. The first time I saw it I think I bawled so hard I didn't absorb it all. It makes me cry to watch it but it also brings me some comfort as it keeps Michael alive for me. I get to see him, hear him talk and that means so much as talking was always so important for us. I was okay in the morning. A friend called and offered her condolences. She said she knew that because we had such a short time together that she left me alone but did think of me often. I also talked to the wife of one of Michael's friends and that helped as well. I was feeling very lethargic today and it was really hard to do anything.

In the afternoon Jeremy and I watched the movie Havana and the movie's scenes brought back all the happy memories of our trip to Cuba.

> *From: Cynda*
> *To: Mae*
> *Date: Thursday, August 21, 2008 9:27 AM*
> *Subject: A wish*
>
> *Dear Mae and Dick:*
> *Have been thinking of you.*
> *I have been dreaming of Michael night after night but I cannot remember in detail what has occurred. All I know is that he is there and it gives me comfort. I did dream one night a few days ago that we were shopping for groceries*

*and he was well, without oxygen and walking comfortably.
The first several nights I didn't dream about him and was
desperate for it.*

*I can't possibly understand all of what you are going
through as everyone has a different relationship with each
person. All I know is how I feel.*

*I just wanted to let you know that I watched the DVD that
Michael made last night with Molly. She, Baree and Asia
saw it on Sunday.*

*I really hope that you and Dick will watch it as it brought
me comfort. It made me cry hysterically but in the end it
brought me comfort which is what Michael intended it to
do. He worried so much about everyone and this was his
last gift of love to all of us.*

*I have not been able to sleep in my bed till last night after
watching the CD. It wasn't until the middle of the night but
it was a start for me. I don't know if I will ever be able to
start off going to sleep in my own bed ever again.*

*I also wanted to share the email below with you as that
was what I sent to my friends and family. This later
became part of my eulogy.*

Take care.

Love

Cynda

CHAPTER SIXTEEN
REMEMBERING MICHAEL

August 23, 2008

Today we had Michael's Celebration of Life. It was held at Sally and William's house and about 50 to 60 people attended. As it started at 3:00 pm quite a few people came then as they could not stay later in the evening. Michael's long time business partner Henry and his wife flew in from Calgary which was kind of them. His parents did not attend but all of his immediate family members and some cousins were there.

Matt ended up buying Michael's car and on the day of the Celebration he picked me up and I cried when I got into the car. It was surreal to be back in that car and Michael wasn't driving it. The little Hawaiian girl that Michael had mounted on the dashboard of the car had already been removed by his dad and now sat on the box that holds Michael's ashes.

My dear friend Melanie came which meant so much to me. She was so supportive and I was most grateful that she was there.

I gave my eulogy and quite a few people spoke, Matt, Mary Anne, two of Michael's old friends Charles and Ian, cousins Kailey and Rhea. Michael was larger than life and was loved by all that knew him. I was thanked by so many for being there for Michael and helping him with everything. His cousin Kailey also added that she was sure glad it was me and that when she met me she was really happy.

Dinner was potluck and everyone was asked to bring a dish that Michael liked. I made the salad we liked from the Golden Boot Cafe, the Jamie Oliver tomato and oregano chicken dish, Michael's salsa, peanut butter chocolate chip cookies and chocolate chip cookies. I also brought Truffles and a bottle of red wine that had been Michael's.

Other dishes were lime pie, pork chops with special sauce, buns from New Town Bakery, lasagna, soya sauce chicken and barbeque pork and Chilliwack corn. There was much too much food. Michael would have been pleased by the food, turn out and speeches.

I love him so much and miss him terribly. I feel like I have a big hole in my heart.

At least last night I dreamt about Michael and this time I could see him in my dream. In my dream, I brought him sweet and sour meat on rice (not one of his favs).

Yesterday morning when I woke up I knew that I had dreamed about Michael but did not see him. I felt his presence strongly and felt better.

August 27, 2008

I received the following email from Erik, a long time friend of Michael's who I never had the chance to meet. It brought me comfort then and does today.

Hi Cynda

I hope you are well. I just wanted to write to you about the message of life that you posted about Michael. It was the most beautiful, loving and sincere message about someone that I have ever read. You loved Michael very much. He always knew it also. It was very comforting to Michael to know that you remained by his side. He was blessed to be surrounded by so many loving friends and family.

Throughout all these years Michael and I have managed to remain good friends even though we did not see each other as much as we would have liked. Michael will remain one of my very good friends that made a difference. I am a very lucky man to have known Michael for the very short time in life that we were friends. I will keep your statement forever. I have read it many times and every time I read it, it makes me feel a little more at peace inside. My heart and love go out to you Cynda. I pray that Our Lord take good care of you and give you the strength that you need. Sincerely and always your friend.............

September 7, 2008

I met with Molly at the corner of Broadway and Commercial as we would be going to spread some of Michael's ashes at Langview Golf Course. This was where Michael learned to play golf at the tender age of 7. This was also the place where he first met a dear golfing buddy back in 1989 who became a life-long friend.

Langview was always special to Michael and last year he and I walked the course. He pointed out all the various holes and the special memories he had of them. He also pointed out the grove of trees where he had planted some herbal seeds and managed to cultivate a crop.

After walking the course we stopped at the little restaurant and sat outside and shared a pop. It was a nice warm day. A man was sitting outside as well and he was smoking. Michael asked him to stop smoking or move over, I cannot remember which. Anyways they ended up talking and Michael was so candid. He told him about his cancer and said that the guy should quit. He said he knew he should quit as he had just recently lost a close relative and he should know better. He talked to Michael for a little longer and thanked him for his honestly and left. I was never so proud of Michael. He didn't have to do this and people can often be hostile when given unsolicited advice such as this. Smoking is after all a touchy subject.

Anyways, Molly and I went to go to pick up Dick and take him to Langview. Baree, Mae, and a group of Michael's golf buddies were already there playing golf.

It was great to see Dick as it had probably been about two weeks. I know I last saw him on the Sunday before the Celebration. I hugged him and it felt very good. I said to Molly later that I guess Michael's dad, for me, is like the grandpa I never had. I love him and didn't even realize it as I was too busy caring for Michael.

Molly, Dick and I joined the others. Sometime later Aunty Shirley and Uncle Tim joined us.

Michael wanted some ashes spread on the Bunker on the 10th hole.

Aunty Shirley had brought a long stemmed pale cream rose wrapped in cellophane. She handed the rose to Mae who placed it standing straight up on the ledge of the bunker. Together his parents placed two golf balls as well as two tees on the same ledge. One of the tees was the indestructible type that Michael loved so much. His parents then spread some of Michael's ashes.

Mae, Aunty Shirley and I were sitting on a bench nearby. Mae was to my right and Aunty Shirley to my left. Dick was wandering around I think and all the others were gathered by Mae. Several of his closest golfing buddies came and they wished us well and walked off.

I was talking to Aunty Shirley and happened to look to my left and glanced at the bunker with the items placed there to honour Michael. Suddenly without warning I heard the snap of cellophane and saw the rose rise up in the air, not very high but definitely up and then go straight down onto the ground to lay on its side right next to the bunker. It made me believe in life after death as it had to be Michael moving the rose quickly so that we would not draw any attention to ourselves. I couldn't see him but he was standing there and snatched the rose and flicked it to the ground. The force with which it happened made me think that it took a lot of energy to make it happen as well as it was done quickly to not draw any attention. Before Michael died he had called the golf club and asked about spreading some of his ashes there. He was told that it wasn't allowed but as long as no attention was drawn to the spreading it could be done. He reminded us more than once to make sure we did the spreading discretely and did not draw any attention.

Witnessing this made me so happy and brought me great comfort. Michael was close by.

His dad later picked the rose up as he did not hear what we said and put the rose back in its original spot. This time it stayed.

Aunty Shirley had heard the sharp snap of the cellophane and commented that there was no wind and so it couldn't have been that. I was the only one that witnessed this and Molly believes that only I was supposed to see it so that I would know that Michael was there. I am sobbing uncontrollably as I write this. I am so very overwhelmed and miss him so much. I cannot believe he is gone and sometimes tell myself that he is not and I guess he really isn't gone as he will forever be in my heart and my soul. I had told Michael this many times that this was and is the depth of my love for him.

We continued on the course and everyone played the 11th and 12th holes. They all knew that the 13th hole was significant to me and Michael. He would often drive to the back side of the 13th hole, park, get out of the car and just savour the view.

We got to the 13th hole. I had to walk up a flight of stairs to get there. The golfers went to the hole to play. I walked to the spot that Michael and I always went to see the view and more importantly where he proposed to me on June 23rd.

CHAPTER SEVENTEEN
LIVING WITH GRIEF

September 8, 2008

I started counselling today at Crossroads Hospice Society and I have been loaned a book called Widow to Widow which so far helps. The counsellor talked to me for two hours and was most supportive. She also showed me a wonderful story about dragonflies which explains death to children. I find it helps to give adults some solace as well.

I am exhausted and drained of energy; I feel like I cannot go on and just cannot cope.

September 9, 2008

I woke up very confused. I didn't get the best sleep and almost feel like I didn't dream about Michael at all. In the back of mind I know I did though.

I have been struggling a great deal emotionally over the last few days. I miss Michael even more and it hurts so much more than I ever thought it could. I hold it together for the most part during the day and then I lose it when I get home. It will be a month tomorrow and I am certain that this date as well as many other things are on my mind.

I have been sobbing uncontrollably since I got home and I would think I would have run out of tears by now but haven't. I am listening to a very therapeutic CD of Chinese chanting music. We used to listen to this first thing in the morning with breakfast. I have always enjoyed this CD and find it really comforting.

When I cry it usually starts with thinking about Michael and letting it sink in that he is really gone. That he is really dead and that I cannot touch him anymore and that his ashes are sitting up in my bedroom waiting for a proper container to be stored in. Currently I have some in nice Chinese vase/urn that I have from Dick. The balance of the ashes are in the plastic bag and sits in my nice Chinese box for now. I have been trying to figure out what I want to keep Michael's ashes in. At first I thought about a turtle and then I decided that I would like to keep some in a heart shaped locket. It is just a matter of buying one. In the end I didn't buy a locket as I thought it was too morbid to have his ashes around my neck.

I called and left a message for Lawrence the jewelry guy to please call. I don't think he knows that Michael has died and I will tell him when I talk to him. I expect that Lawrence will know of someone that he can get me what I want. It could even have a Dragonfly on it as I have now found great significance in the dragonfly story and it is ironic that I very recently purchased two dragonfly solar lamps which are set up just outside our front steps. I only bought these 4 or 5 days prior to going to counseling. It is almost another incident of how things just fall into place for us, no longer us but for Michael and I as it always had in the past.

I just cannot believe he is really gone. That is the hardest part. I surround myself with pictures of Michael and I and all I want to do is listen to his voice, sob and look at pictures and talk to him. I tell him all the time how much I miss him and ask how am I supposed to cope without him? I feel like I can't breathe some days. I don't inhale and exhale properly. I feel choked and short of breath. I feel like my chest is tight. Everything hurts. I don't know how I eat, I guess it is emotional and the steroids.

The despair I feel is awful. I force myself to go to work, get dressed and do things. I do at least like to cook and feel the urge to do that still, as well as grocery shop. Running errands gives me a sense of purpose and I like that.

I have wonderful support from some of the ladies at work and for that I am extremely grateful.

The medications are helping and I am not shy about using the Ativan as it really helps.

September 12, 2008

I woke up remembering a dream about Michael for the very first time. Not only that he spoke to me in the dream but I could see him clearly.

I dreamt that he was wearing a fluffy white housecoat. He was bare feet, smiling and happy. He looked the same as he did before he died except he was a little slimmer, had no oxygen tubes and was breathing without any problems. He had the housecoat tied with a belt and was holding an open bag of No Name ketchup chips. He has just come from above (Heaven) in a circular motion as if he was coming down a slide and had just arrived at the main floor. He asked me what took me so long to get home/here? He was really happy to see me and it was wonderful to finally hear him talk in my dream. He said more but I couldn't remember what after I woke up.

I have been trying very hard not to dwell in the "How can I possibly live without him or I can't believe he's gone" as well as all negative feelings that make me feel distraught. I realize that I must not allow myself to continue like this as it is no good for me. I know that I have gone a bit overboard with pictures but I feel really good surrounded by all the pictures. Also it is an easy enough remedy should I feel that later there are too many, I can always pack them up. Right now I just have to do what feels good.

I was thinking more and more about why Michael and I met and I came to the conclusion that we didn't meet just to only be together for 1 year and 7 months. We met because we are soul mates and we were always destined to meet and would be together for eternity. I questioned why I was and am so concerned that I won't find him again one day. It was an unrealistic fear and not one that I should have. Michael and I talked often about being together forever. I also reminded myself that although his physical body is no longer on this earth, his spirit is with me and he is in my heart and soul. It has given me a feeling of calmness and I feel more reassured that we will be together forever.

This is where I need to have faith. I forget and get caught up with grieving and sobbing and being so sad. Things that threw me off big time were that my cell phone stopped working the day Michael died. Michael never said I love you in any of the many voicemail messages that I saved, both on my phone at home and at work. He didn't in the DVD. He only said so in the voice memos that were on my phone and are now lost. One of his messages was that he loved his glamour pussy so much.

I started to exercise more and I went to yoga three times. I want to cry quite often. I also think of how happy Michael would be that I am back to practicing. I have also been logging a lot of mileage with running errands and walking.

I am sad less and the despair is less and reading the Widow to Widow book helps.

Tonight I used the barbeque to prepare dinner. I made grilled peppers, zucchini, mushrooms and lamb chops. Some were perfect, some a little crisper than needed but none were overcooked and they were tasty. Michael would have been pleased. I have finally learned how to use the barbeque properly and safely. I told Jeremy that one of the many things that Michael did for me was that he would teach me things. He taught me to be self-sufficient, even more than I used to be. I find that now when I prepare meals I make much more effort. I care a lot more to do it right and think about the process much more. I am content in my kitchen and it feels really good.

I was always capable, but Michael gave me back my confidence that was decimated after my second marriage ended. I had already regained a great deal of confidence after losing all the weight. I now know that that is where I need to focus. I need to get healthy again. Lose the weight and learn to live my old life from before I met Michael but to live that life with the changes to my life because of Michael. I want to be healthy and fit again, to exercise and excel. I want to run a half marathon next year. I want a flat belly again. I know I can do it. I want to be good and great at yoga. I just have to decide and believe and follow through. I have done it before and I know I can do it again. I had to put my health and fitness on hold as Michael was so sick that I needed to spend every moment with him. He and I knew that it was a temporary sacrifice. How I wish that we could have had a miracle and that I would still have him today. If he had beaten cancer we would have gotten back to routines and we would have been healthy.

Exercise can be an obsession until I reach my goal but friends and fun will factor into the picture more. I will make time for friends and friendships. I put too much off before to work out and isolated myself.

A co-worker said something so nice to me today. She said that she was thinking how amazing it was that he was so positive and took the chance to find someone. He could have retreated from life. I am ever so grateful that I followed my heart all the way and didn't lose out or run from the opportunity of falling for the love of my life. For that I am truly grateful and I need to always remember that.

September 14, 2008

I met up with Lawrence and he sold me a cedar box designed by his mom, a local native artist, in which I put some of Michael's ashes. I also bought silver hummingbird earrings to put with the ashes.

For Michael, Love Cynda

September 16, 2008

This had to be the first day that I felt happy since
Michael died. I am surprised that I had a day like
that so soon. I brought Tiramisu and Sex in a Pan to
the office and thanked everyone for their kindness and
compassion. I still have to go to the bathroom and
cry, usually once a day, sometimes twice. I also know
when to take the Ativan when I feel like an attack of
anxiety and stress is coming on. I get agitated and
cannot relax or inhale or exhale properly. I still
and expect to be doing this for some time, keep going
on in my head that I cannot believe that Michael is
really gone. I know he is gone and that he has died
and that he is dead. I don't want and like to use lame
words like passed away. It is too soft for the immense
pain that I feel. He is dead and I am broken. I miss
him so much. Although it was a really good day for me
it was sad because I always shared everything with him
and actually I forget that I still do. I don't have to
always journalise it although I should continue to do
this as well as talk to Michael. Sometimes I don't get
to my bedroom until I am exhausted. I need to spend
more quiet time in here I think. I get myself into
a frenzy with being constantly busy so that I avoid
thinking. It is also my way of avoiding dealing with
feeling the pain.

Sunday night I don't remember dreaming about Michael
at all. It felt very empty. I think I dreamt about
laundry but am not certain. I used to always dream
about doing laundry when I was stressed. Last night I
did dream about him but couldn't remember anything. It
is really strange how your mind processes things.

233

September 20, 2008

I have less reliance on Ativan.

Before going to bed I cried and talked to Michael to please come to me in my dreams as I need him so much. He did. I don't recall most of it but he was there. In my dreams we talked and kissed a lot.

When he died, I didn't just lose him, I lost my way of life. I lost the home I shared with him in Richmond and I was not part of his family anymore. I no longer had the same relationship with his children, I lost his parents as they were of course overcome with grief, and I lost my cat, Spyder as I loved him too. My day to day life had changed. Everyone still had their person that they leaned on. I lost my person and lost my balance.

Maybe I would have felt better if I was still at the apartment but I could not bear to go back there after he died.

When I woke up I felt like he was here with me and I felt much calmer and very comforted.

The week went by very quickly and I had some very tough times. I cried lots and just went with the flow. I did what I needed to feel good and didn't worry about anything else but doing what feels good.

I have been cooking a lot lately and I know Michael would be happy with that. I take much more care when I do cook now. I made curried beef on Thursday night and on Friday night I made spaghetti and meatballs. I used two cans of plum tomatoes, threw in a jar of chunky seasoned sauce and added Costco meatballs along with basil, bay leaves, chili peppers, garlic, onions, mushrooms, zucchini, sage and black pepper. Sons were very happy with pasta and ate all of it. I grilled Jeremy several times to confirm that yes, it really does taste a lot better than how I used to make pasta sauces. I was quite pleased with myself. I looked at the treasured recipe from the small town restaurant that Michael had shared with me and picked out the seasonings that I should use.

Honey, I miss you so very much. I tell you that all the time because that is how I feel. It is like a part of my heart has been ripped out. My other half is not here and I am lost. I am starting to find my way a bit better but am still very lost.

I really miss your kids too and that is tough. They are both dealing with losing their Dad and I have called a few times and left messages. I cannot fully understand what they are going through. They had a wonderful relationship with their dad.

It finally hit me the other night, I think Wednesday, that WE ARE ALL STRUGGLING and I always knew it wasn't just me, I just felt like I felt it the most, as I was Mrs. Flet and I am missing you. Everyone has someone else and I don't. I love you so much and I am scared of trying to live a life without you. I know I did it before (as Jeremy said to me) but after loving you, living without you is a whole different ballgame.

September 22, 2008

I went for my yearly mammogram. I even wished that I might get breast cancer so that I could die and be with Michael. How awful that I wanted that even for a moment when there are so many women and men diagnosed with this disease only to succumb to it. I had better be careful with what I wish. I feel such despair some days and today is one of them. Mondays are always hard. I won't get the reward of seeing Michael after work. I miss him terribly and nothing at this point can ease the loneliness of missing him.

> *I told Molly today that every day I talk to you. Sometimes when I arrive home, I go straight to my bedroom as that was my habit when I was with you.*
>
> *I used to come home to the apartment, go to the bedroom to find you or I would find you in the office. Sometimes you were such a brat as you would sit quietly in the office and wait for me to come to you. If I had groceries I would put them away first and then I would go to the bathroom and freshen up and then come to find you.*
>
> *I am grateful for all the times that I reached out and touched you as you slept. I just needed to have my hand or body part touch a part of you. I would always remind myself that I need to savour and soak up all of this now as one day I wouldn't be able to have your touch. How I wish I had never ever stopped touching you for a moment. I would think this as I sat next to you and would cuddle with you or would hold your hand or lean on you. Oh, the agony is just unbelievable. I have to as I know I must let myself cry and say to you all of what I feel for if I don't I will never be able to heal and move forward. I will never in essence move on as there is no moving on for me. You were and are the Love of My Life and will always be.*

I feel certain I will not have another man in my life as Michael was the best and I will not settle. He was everything I could have ever dreamed or hoped to find. I had my mental checklist: Divorced, independent, had children that were teens or grown, divorced for several years, at least 5, capable of .looking after himself, smart, funny, attractive and loved me more than I loved him. A guy that had been beaten up a little emotionally by other women so that he would really, really appreciate me. I just fucking forgot to ask for a man that was healthy and would live for a long time.

My heart aches when I think about living a long life without Michael and because of that I don't dare go past the next day. I am truly living one day at a time now. The counselor says that dying teaches us about living and that is so very true. Michael taught me so much. I was always so scared of cancer and also about dying. I have gone through all of this with him now and so I am no longer as scared of dying. Cancer still scares the shit out of me but I have an awareness now as we lived with the disease.

When someone is dying it brings out strange things in people. People who you were not close to, suddenly want to spend time with you while others have a difficult time and do not come to see you. One of his old friends did not visit him and was heartbroken after Michael died. I think part of it is that people tend to avoid talking and thinking about death. Maybe if there were more conversations before death was imminent we would be better at handling it. Life and death does after all, go hand in hand.

After Michael died one person asked if an autopsy was going to be performed on him. Another friend of his asked me when his Will was going to be read.

Michael and I each had our struggles with his dying. Although we hoped for a miracle, we knew the odds were that the cancer would eventually end his life. He struggled with spending money. He did not usually want to buy things as his time to use them would be limited but he would invest money in experiences. Travel was something we both adored and spending money to travel and enjoy life were easy choices.

When we were first together Michael bought what he wanted with his money but as time progressed and he outlived his initial prognosis, I recall his being angry and sad about spending money on a roasting pan. I said I would buy it as I wanted a good one. As he would not be able to use it for as long it made sense to not spend much money. I have a slight glimpse into this way of thinking as I grow older and think about how many years I may use something now.

As I struggled with my role as Michael's partner/caregiver and that as mom to my sons, I often felt torn. Because he was dying, I wanted to spend every moment with him.

I talked to Michael a few times that one of my biggest fears was that I would die before he does. I said to him that I could have an accident, one never knows. It horrified me to think that this was a possibility and then I would have sacrificed all this time to care for and be with him, only to deprive myself, family and friends of me. What a horrible thing to think about.

Many of his friends and some family had said that it was too bad that we did not find each other earlier. I appreciated the sentiment, but I would not have been ready for Michael then. I honestly don't believe he would have been ready for me either. I had to go through many experiences in my life to become who I am and he was, naturally, greatly affected by his cancer diagnosis and it made him the man that I fell madly in love with.

I had a hysterectomy in 2002, lost 94 lbs during 2003 and 2004 and kept it off for over 2 years. I became fit, practiced yoga, and became a runner which was a dream come true. I had always liked running from the time that Andrew was a baby, but could never get the stamina to run for more than one or two blocks. After starting to run, I could run 5k, 10k and even a half marathon. It was pretty amazing for me to achieve these dreams.

If I hadn't had my own cancer scare (doctors found pre-cancer cells and so I had a hysterectomy) I wouldn't have become who I became. I realized at the time just how lucky I was that it wasn't one, cancer, two, terminal cancer. I knew that I had to do something to change my life as this was a warning sign and if I was going to be stupid and not appreciate and be grate-ful for this warning sign/wake up call then I would deserve what was due to me in the future.

I do truly believe this which is a good thing so that there is no lamenting about what could have been. I had to have gone through my own transformation, getting fit and healthy, becoming an athlete really. I climbed the Grouse Grind some 60 times in 3 years which is pretty amazing for a woman that used to be 218 lbs. Eventually the number exceeded 100 climbs.

I guess I need to remember that now as I am over-wrought, exhausted and depressed; I don't eat horribly as I am eating balanced. I would like to eat lighter and healthier and am working towards that. I know and have been told that dieting at this time is not the smartest idea. What I was told to do is to eat three meals a day. I know that my immune system has taken a huge beating as a result of Michael's death and I need to give it time to recover. Since he died, I had been on one course of antibiotics and two courses of prednisone. I am also on a diuretic for high blood pressure which at least went back to normal in the middle of last week. High blood pressure is not a problem I have had previously. I am on the Ativan in the afternoon and at bedtime. It is ironic to be on some of the same medications as Michael. I am certain that there are days when Morphine would just hit the spot but I know I won't go for that. I also am careful not to numb my pain with alcohol either. It would be so very easy to become an alcoholic right now. I could just obliterate how I feel.

It is now 12:45 am and the Ativan has really kicked in. I am dizzy and spinny with exhaustion and so it is definitely time to go to sleep.

Love you so much honey. Hope things in heaven are what you had hoped for. Remember not too many midnight snacks (but I guess in heaven there are no calories) so just go for it. Don't forget about me okay. I worry that we will be apart too long and you will forget about me. I know I am just being silly as you really really loved me lots and I know I will never get that again.

Makes me extra sad. Love you dear and I hope you come to me in my dreams tonight and hold me close.

Love you, Mrs. Flet.

For Michael, Love Cynda

September 25, 2008

It has been tougher and tougher lately. This week has been full of tears. I forced myself to visualize Michael yesterday with fluffy angel wings, looking happy and sitting at a table playing cards with his cousin who had passed away a short time before I met Michael. I could visualize him wearing his favorite watch, checking it and making comments that I am sure taking a long time to get there.

I miss you honey. I say this to you daily and generally several times as it is so hard. It hurts so much. Some days I just don't know how to keep going. I never think past a few days. Although things are planned for next month I don't think too much about them as I really try hard to stick to one day at a time right now because it makes it bearable. I dreamed about Michael the last two nights and yesterday was very strong but I cannot remember anything just that he was there. Those are the gist of my dreams.

I also keep running into people I know and then when they ask me how I am I tell them that you died and how rough it is.

I feel really, really lonely some days although I am not alone. There are lots of people around. It is just that you are the one that I need and miss. I know that I should journal more and I need to write more about our life together and all the important aspects of it.

I want to plan the Pitt spreading but that seems to be overwhelming. I know everyone is grieving too. I feel like I have it the worst as I spent every moment with you and now I am so totally lost.

Today I really felt despair and it crossed my mind to take too many Ativans and then I thought about my kids finding me dead and there is no way I could ever do that. I just need to put one foot in front of the next, breathe and take it slow. I can't do it all and am going to stick to just doing what feels good.

I love you my darling and I wish this was just a horrific nightmare that I would finally wake up from. Maybe that is what life on earth is, just a dream of sorts. I do believe it is a prequel and I fear how long I will have here without you. That is the part that scares me the most.

September 26, 2008

After I read what Michael's requirements were in a partner, I realize just now finally, that I met all that he was looking for too. I guess I always knew that. He would always say that things just come to us easily and naturally and that we don't have to work at it.

Very early in our relationship Michael was driving north on Garden City Road and he talked about living together. I made some comment and he was shocked and was goofy and said "What you already decided that you don't want to live with me." I said no, that I would consider it or something to that effect. We were very new but looking back now I can see that he really didn't like to be apart. I didn't either. I always missed him when we were not together and that is why I am so lost and so profoundly sad.

He would often meet me at the bus stop even though it was only about a block from his apartment. Sometimes we would just sit at the Starbucks and have something to drink before going home.

Later on we looked at our living situation many times. He wanted me to live with him as I did too, but it was a struggle. I had so many belongings as well as my two sons. I did seriously consider selling my townhouse and we also talked and looked a bit at buying a place in Richmond. In the end it was just not feasible as I wouldn't sell the townhouse unless I could get a condo and be ahead a fair amount financially.

September 26, 2008

I am angry. I feel intense rage inside of me. I am exploding. I am sad, I am mad and I am downright pissed off. A former co-worker is getting married and I just said goodbye to the love of my life some six weeks ago.

I am so sad and I miss you so much. Fridays are so fucking hard and I can't take it. Little things are making me snap. Jeremy not listening pisses me off. Andrew not refilling the Brita makes me insane, ditto for not closing the bathroom cupboard all the way or leaving the mirrored cupboard partly open. I have no tolerance and I am mad.

I am so sick of Jeremy whining that he is tired. I think he should have no tv and no computer for a week since he is so tired. I am going to make the kid go to bed early for the next few nights. I am sick of a 16 year old, healthy and yet so lazy. It drives me nuts. You pushed and pushed yourself so hard so that you could be here for all of us honey and it took so much out of you. I know that. I miss you so much. It is so tough and I am dying inside. My heart is broken and I don't know where the pieces are. I feel shattered and

*devastated. I am overwhelmed by the pain of not having
you here to talk to daily. Why the hell didn't I spend every
second with you. I should have done that. I did do my
best to savour every moment as I knew that one day this
day would come. I just was never prepared. Still never
prepared for how empty and dead I would feel.*

September 28, 2008

Yesterday I went to Stanley Park with Abby and her
Emma for a brisk walk around the park. The day was
incredibly beautiful and it did me a world of good.
Errands at the mall afterwards and got home around
3:00 pm. I took out all my winter clothes and put away
all of summer. I did laundry, cleaned, tidied up, ran
up and down the stairs with great frequency and later
fell asleep in a chair in the basement.

I went to a craft market with my friend and we had
a really fun time. Feeling less sad but still sad. I
find I get angry and cranky at the boys. Other times I
get impatient and intolerant and then I cry and say
sorry. Need that Ativan and time to heal. I am cooking
a lot and there is a lot less crying due to my keeping
extremely busy. I am living at a frenetic pace again.

October 1, 2008

*I am sad. I miss you honey. I had dinner tonight with Baree
and Molly. I start to see some of you in him now. I gave
Molly the Cuba picture that I had blown up as well as
the picture of you practicing yoga. That is a picture that I
treasure so much as you were at so much peace at that
time. We were so newly in love when we were in Cuba.*

*I told Molly all my fears and feelings today. I told her how
I would have kidnapped your body after you died. I also*

noticed today that the picture of you with Spyder that I took at the hospice is gone from my camera. How could that possibly happen when I protect the pictures on the camera so they are not accidentally deleted. Luckily I already saved a copy to the computer and had a print made. Molly says it was you. I am convinced you are sending me messages by doing this. I love you so much honey and I can't bear to live without you some days. It is just so tough. I went to counseling yesterday in a group and I bawled my head off. I cried more for the others and what they are going through. Not just for how much I miss you and how terribly heartbroken I am. I don't think I could have missed you any more than I do right now. You were my everything, please hold me and make me feel safe. I need you so much.

October 5, 2008

Dear Michael, I thought about you so very much last night. I went to see Hilary Hahn play with the Vancouver Symphony. Wished that you were there and I guess you were there, just not physically. I love you so much. I miss you terribly and the ache and sadness are so overwhelming.

October 6, 2008

Tonight I had dinner with Mary Anne and it was really nice to see her. I also got to see Alexandra honey and she was looking well. School is going well and she is very busy. She is glowing and I am certain it is because she is in love. Mary Anne says that she spends lots of time with her boyfriend.

We talked about you of course. How you wanted all of us to be happy and that you wanted us all to be healthy. Mary

Anne has seen the DVD and it gave her comfort. I am so glad. She has been reminding the kids that they shouldn't wait too long and should see it. Spyder looks great. He is firmer than before and I really missed him. He is noisy too and talks lots now. He doesn't like to be cuddled much anymore though. Mary Anne says that he will come to sit with you but doesn't like the cuddling. I am sure that he misses you but I am happy that you have your Tea, baby girl (the family dog who had to be put down after Michael died) with you now. I just have to learn how to live without you each day. Mary Anne says that she has a hard time dealing with the fact that you are gone. I feel that way too. I told her that I was never worried about you not being okay but I worried about how I was going to go on living without you. I talked about how my whole world has changed. I told her about group and the other counselor. I miss you terribly and it hurts so much. I told her that I have such a hard time without you but that the people in group have had it even tougher. Said that even though I was only with you for 1 ½ years I loved you like I had been with you for 30 years and that some people had really been with partners for 30 years. I also told her about the lady that lost her parent and then lost her husband (unexpectedly) all within 6 months.

Eric wasn't there. Wished he was. I miss him a lot. He is part of you as is Alexandra. I wish so much that I could have had a baby with you. I know that is silly as we were much too old to have kids but oh honey, I love you so much. I guess I am making up for not crying yesterday. Right now I am sobbing. I cried a bit talking with Mary Anne but it was good talking to her. She was your first and I was your last. That is how I will always see us.

For Michael, Love Cynda

October 10, 2008

I went to group counseling earlier this week at a local hospital and got a few things out of my system. It hurts like hell and lately I have been very low on energy, just exhausted. Tom and Edane are wonderful. Tom is with the palliative care and Edane with the local hospice. They read some poetry written by C.S. Lewis who lost his wife and I have ordered the book. You were my husband in every way and I am so very lost without you. Tom also spoke about how it is normal for us to wish and wish that the person we lost could be alive.

I have been lazier about turning on the computer of late. I have cried less, felt numb and dead inside. I couldn't even be happy on the day that Margy and Marc were coming. I was just sad. I miss you so much honey. I even try to tell myself sometimes that I wouldn't have been able to cope with years with you but I know that that is a lie as I would have been happy with you for years. I feel so ripped off that I waited so long for you and I didn't get to have you for longer. I miss you terribly and I am just overwhelmed with pain.

Today it is two months since you died and I had a really good talk with Margy about you. I am so broken and it hurts so much. I sob uncontrollably some days and I just don't know how I will go on.

Saw my family doctor for a follow up yesterday and I am on my third course of antibiotics and am to continue with the diuretic and Ativan. Blood pressure is really good. He said that the diuretic is also good to get rid of excess bloating caused by the prednisone.

I went to Superstore today and I don't think I have been in a Save On Foods since you died. I have been to Safeway and I want to cry when I go to Costco or to Superstore. I have a really hard time at Superstore as I remember all the times we were there for cranberry juice, soda, pop and the time you picked out a 2 buck chuck or the rack of lamb and how I have not eaten any fake crab since shortly after I met you.

I had a nice time in Gastown with Margy and Marc and thought about you often. We looked at t-shirts with native art. I took Margy and Marc to yoga and then we went for dim sum at Imperial Chinese Seafood Restaurant. (That's the restaurant where I picked up dim sum for Michael after his brain tumor surgery.) I looked at native necklaces to try to find one with a hummingbird but didn't find one. We walked around Canada Place, went to Salmagundi, Pacific Centre and then Margy and Marc went off to her sister's and I went grocery shopping.

Mondays and Fridays are really hard for me, as are Sundays. Today was hard and I am really glad I took the day off. I would just be so sad. I miss you so much. I know I will never get over you and I guess I am not supposed to. You just learn to live with the loss and continue with living.

I told a friend that I am doing everything that I am supposed to do to cope. I am going to group and individual counselling as well as lots of yoga, walking and really wanting to run. I may try tomorrow afternoon as I sprinted home today and it was okay. Actually maybe not as okay as the bones in my feet ache a bit but then we walked lots today.

For Michael, Love Cynda

I love you honey. I really, really hope you come to me in my dreams and kiss me and hold me. I miss the mornings when you would hug me and twist your lips sideways and kiss me.

October 11, 2008

I had one of the most difficult and emotionally draining nights. I felt like I had been hit by a truck. I think the realization that I will never see or talk to Michael again is sinking in. I know there are no guarantees I get to see him in the future, I just sure hope I do. I feel broken, distraught and in agony. I took an Ativan this am and feel like I need another but I want to have a glass of wine tonight so I don't think so.

October 12, 2008

Tonight Jeremy and I went to Mary Anne's house for Thanksgiving dinner. It also happened to be Asia's birthday, I met her mom Ava. Charles, Helen, Tessa and Vince were there. The first thing Vince said to me was that Spyder was missing for an entire week, I just about started crying because I believed him. Eric looked well but Alexandra looked tired. I gave Alexandra a birthday card with a 5 x 7 print of Michael taken on August 8th.

I talked to Eric about the Vedder River as his mom wants to be there for the spreading of ashes, and I want to be there as well. I don't recall what happened but I never made the trip.

Dinner was really nice and I did not realise until we were almost leaving that Michael's dinner table was in the living room. It had no table cloth on it and I didn't recognize it. Charles made a wonderful turkey, Mary Anne made stuffing, there was salad, swiss chard, mixed veggies, gravy, and the usual. Dessert was Helen's key lime pie, sex in a pan, pumpkin pie and Tessa's apple crumble.

I talked to Helen a lot, and she said that it was Michael's time, and that it was like he knew it was time. I told Helen that if I had to be off longer from work than the end of August, I would have had to make a decision. She said we were lucky not to have had to stay in the hospice longer. I said I had expected to be there for months. She said it was like Michael planned it all. I told her that I had gone back to work at the beginning of September.

It was really wonderful to see everyone. I had been anxious that I would cry a lot and I was fine until I talked to Spyder. I told Spyder that I miss him a lot but that it was good that he was here as Eric, Alexandra and Mary Anne needed him.

Eric drove us home as he was helping to bring Michael's living room carpet over to my place.

October 15, 2008

Yesterday was the third week of group counselling. I didn't cry as much this time and talked about Thanksgiving and how it was tough with Michael's parents and Baree and that I had dinner with Baree and Molly about a week and a half ago.

I also shared the golf club ash spreading and my cell phone story.

For Michael, Love Cynda

I felt better after hearing what another person said. He said that there was no baggage from their 45 years together. When I think of that I feel better. Michael and I talked everything out and so we had no baggage either. I do question how I could have done more, saved him and been there for him more. Although my logical and practical side tells me I couldn't have done anything more.

I talked about how I wanted to do the Nike race and that I wanted to run it but wasn't in any shape to do so and decided I wanted to volunteer. I had talked to Michael about volunteering and he told me that he preferred that I didn't do it. I said to him that I guess there would be an orientation and then more time would be involved and so I said I wouldn't do it. In the end because he died, I was able to volunteer. When I was there that night I was enjoying myself and then I felt guilty that I was there because he had died and I would have preferred to have been at the hospice instead. (Since that time I have done many things, going to the symphony, yoga at the festival with Melanie, walking through Gastown and going down stairs that I know I could not have done with Michael or without him if he were still here.)

It feels like he died when he did so that I could do these things and I felt guilty. Talking to Helen on Sunday night helped as well, as she said it was just Michael's time.

I am grateful that I have contact with the kids and with Mary Anne, and Molly. They are the most important people to me. All the other friends of Michael's are bonuses to me. He made sure I was well looked after.

It was after work and I was struggling to decide whether I wanted to go home or to the mall. I called Jeremy and as I was panting he asked me if I was okay. I told him that I wasn't and that I was having a hard time. I told him of my struggle to decide what to do. He asked me what did I want to do, what did I want? I said that I want Michael alive and without cancer and I want to grow old with him. That's what I want. I got off the phone, kept crying and walked home.

Margy got home. She knocked on the door and we hugged and I cried. I talked to her about how I felt.

I had vivid dreams last night that Michael was still alive. No oxygen tubes though as he said it didn't help at all. He was dying in my dream. He called me on my cell to say something to me. I can't exactly recall what it was now but it was crystal clear in my dream. He said something about he was dying now or it's time or I can't breathe.

I said I would be right there and I was. He was struggling to breathe and I knew he was dying. We were in a bedroom. His mom was there but in another room and she was animated and talking to someone. There was happy chatter coming from them.

He was wearing a grey t-shirt. I don't remember holding him but was sitting with him or at least very close to him. I know that something happened and that I wasn't in the room and then Michael died. I came back and found he had died. It felt okay in my dream. It was like Michael was telling me that it was okay that I wasn't there when he died, that I had to be elsewhere or he couldn't have died. He needed to do it without me in the room.

I also dreamt it was Christmas and Jocelan was making CDs on the laptop. Lots of CDs as I was explaining to her that when the case popped open then it was time to add another CD. I remember getting more CDs for her. It felt like we were in my room but the room was too big. The Christmas tree was out. It was in the middle of what looked like a living room. Jocelan had gotten it out. In my dream Michael had died on Christmas Eve. I knew it was Christmas but not what day. It did not feel like Christmas day.

No Ativan last night as I wanted to drink tonight with Margy. I had scotch and she had red wine. I have never been a scotch drinker. It only started because Michael had a bottle of scotch and as he was never a drinker it was full. When we were together and there was a death, I needed to drink something really strong and so I would drink some scotch. I started to call it the death scotch. Thankfully, many years later the bottle is still not empty.

October 16, 2008

It is Alexandra's birthday today and I hope that despite her Dad not being here that she is having a good day. I know he wanted us to be happy but I feel bad sometimes when I am happy. I guess I feel like I should be sad forever because he is not next to me anymore. I have to remember that he is no longer next to me physically but he will always been in my heart.

I went to Whistler with Margy and Marc yesterday. We had a really nice time. I thanked them for making me go with them and spoiling me. I was worried about going as I didn't know if I could have a good time and I didn't want to bring them down. I just felt so sad. A change of scenery was really good for me and it would have been what Michael would have wanted for me.

A few interesting things happened on this trip. We went to the visitor information yesterday and the person we talked to was named Michael. The guy that worked next to him was also named Michael. Later, an hour or so after, we heard a woman calling for someone and she was yelling out Michael.

We went to an aboriginal cultural centre the next day. It had only opened up this past summer. When I was in Hawaii with Michael we talked about the Polynesian Cultural Centre and how wonderful it was for all the cultures. We wondered why there was nothing in Vancouver when there should be, so I was quite happy to find this place. I told Margy that I wanted to go there and all three of us did and really enjoyed it.

I wanted to paint a rock for Michael. As soon as I found out that there were rocks I wanted to do that. I looked at the chart that they had and there was a picture of a man and a salmon. Both were characters from the Lillooet area which is where Michael's Mom's family had settled. Michael was very proud of his family's long time roots in British Columbia. My grandmother first arrived in Vancouver in 1914 and our family was also one of the early pioneer Chinese families.

I was talking to one of the girl's there and related the story of Michael and my discussion of the cultural centre in Hawaii. I said that he was my fiancé. I told her how happy I was that they have this one here. She asked me when we were going to get married. I told her that he died two months ago as he had cancer and that he had it when I met him. She then shared with me that her fiancé has bipolar disorder and he is also named Michael.

Our trip to Whistler was a much needed escape and after a few days we returned to Vancouver.

October 20, 2008

I went for further counseling at Crossroads Hospice. It went well and I asked the questions I needed to ask. Whether I got the answers I was looking for, I don't know. We toured the hospice and she asked if I wanted to see one of the empty rooms. I told her no. I recoiled at the thought of entering one of the rooms. It was like a page had turned for me. Even though I knew Michael was dead, it reinforced to me that he was in a room just like this one and died. It is still hard to go into the hospice even though this was not the one he was in.

I remember driving past the hospice with Abby shortly after it was built. She commented that each time a light goes out in a room, it means that someone has died. Never in my wildest dreams did I ever expect to meet a man who was terminally ill and then end up living with him both in palliative and hospice care.

I was extremely angry for the rest of the day and mostly in the evening as I was out for much of the day. I was in a rage and the force of the anger scared me. I even went and sat on the front step and cried and stayed outside until I was chilled. I shared this with the group as well.

Edane asked me how I felt when I was talking and crying. I cannot even remember my answer. I remember telling her how tired I have been, just exhausted and that on Saturday I slept 12 hours straight and then had a nap as well.

October 21, 2008

I felt better today than I have since Michael died. I actually felt a bit happy. The weather was nice and I was feeling somewhat normal. I was also feeling apprehensive as I was going to group counselling that night and I didn't want to be sad.

October 22, 2008

There is a hair salon on Grandview Highway that Michael liked to go to for his haircuts. He called it Hong Kong Mary's and we had gone there previously with Jeremy to get a haircut. I was going there today to get my eyebrows threaded as Jeremy wanted to get his hair cut there. The lady that cut his hair (I think it was Mary herself) asked how my boyfriend is. I told her that he died two months ago and she gasped and said "Already!, he looked so good". I told her that he was even eating Chinese BBQ meats the day before he died and that he was in the hospital for just over two weeks. I said he was a really good man. She agreed and said that she was very sorry about that. I guess in some ways going there gave Jeremy and me a fond memory of Michael as he was always so funny when we were there. Joking and laughing. How I miss him. I am a wreck tonight.

November 1, 2008

Our bodies comprise of millions of electrical impulses. Today I received an unexpected email:

Hi

Email from Jake Trout aka Michael

I have no idea how this occurred and it is likely not a coincidence that it was sent on November 1 (111) as 111 is significant for us. No further emails ever came from this account.

Michael and I first spoke by telephone on January 11 (111). His room number at the hospice was 111. The best man at his wedding and where his Celebration of Life was held, died tragically, 1 year, 1 month and 1 day after Michael died. It was on November 11 that I moved into my home, the one that I lived in when I met Michael. I sold that home 11 years later.

Some believe that seeing 11:11 signals a spirit presence. Others also believe that 111 and 1111 are significant. I do not know anything for certain, but they kept showing up in my life.

Numbers are like words for me, I tend to remember them, but I never paid much attention until 111 kept popping up.

November 10, 2008

It has now been three whole months and I cannot believe that I am still breathing, that the sadness didn't kill me. I have been sick for two weeks and so sick of being sick. I had the flu, mostly stomach, the last week of October and then last Wednesday I started to cough and had the chills. I went to see my family doctor on Friday and was prescribed my fourth course of antibiotics. I have been taking NeoCitran and sleeping almost nonstop for two days. Today I feel better but still weak and a bit lightheaded, I took some cough medicine and had a shower and feel much better. I had wanted nothing but to just sleep and forget.

I was doing much better in the early part of last week as I was feeling less distraught and sad. I had just started taking the 5-HTP (this medication increases the production of serotonin) and was also using the therapy light that I had bought. I was going to start dieting and get the weight off as I was so sick of being fat and no longer wanted to be. I want to be fit, healthy and to wear my little dresses again. Because I had been fit and healthy for two years before I met Michael I always feel like my family will think less of him unless I regain my health. I also want to do it for me, but unfortunately to this day it has been a struggle due to ups and downs in life and I am still not back to my previous healthy weight. Michael felt bad at times that my health was compromised as he got sicker.

Lately I have been having so many vivid memories of things and events that have happened over the past year. I said to Jeremy that it is like I am watching episodes from various seasons of a TV show.

I can smell the air. I can taste and feel everything. Memories come bolting back to me when I smell Ivory Snow soap or the fruit shampoo Michael liked. I get sad at Superstore, T & T Supermarket and still cannot bring myself to go to Save On Foods.

About a month or less before Michael died I developed some odd blisters on my left leg. I had thought that maybe a blast of the oxygen from the machine at Michael's had hit my skin and caused the blisters. They were tiny to start and then grew to about the size of a dime after he died. They eventually burst and crusted and then became flat but they left dark spots on my leg and have never gone away. There was no specific treatment just a topical antibiotic. My family doctor sent me to a dermatologist for treatment.

December 2, 2008

I went for a run today and it was the first time since June. I have been thinking about running for several weeks and even longer than that. I never felt like I had the stamina so I did not even try.

Last night I read about a contest in a free local newspaper just before going to bed. It was for their version of The Biggest Loser TV show. I thought about entering the contest and pleading my case. I felt like I really need help to get me back to where I was. I didn't feel strong enough to be able to succeed on my own. I don't know if I can or not. I thought that I could definitely plead my case and that I had a chance of being chosen.

Anyways end of a very hectic day and it was the perfect time for me to go run. I wanted to go so badly that last night I got my clothes ready before bed. I even got out the charger and charged my music device at

work. I was determined not to let anything hold me
back from going.

It was cool and dry and perfect weather for a run. A
little darker than I would like, but I had my cell
with me as well as a flashlight. I plugged myself into
my device and started running at 4:26 pm. I hit the
device to shuffle and skipped the first song which was
Leaving Las Vegas by Sheryl Crow. The next song was
Take Me Home Country Road West Makaha by Iz. I started
to cry. I ran and cried. The next song was a Kenny
Chesney one. Don't know what it was called but it is
Track 5 on the compilation CD made by Michael. It was
like he was here. I kept running and crying. I didn't
know if I would ever run again. I feel so scared sometimes that I will never be able to run or be fit and
thin again. I guess I have gone away from it so far
for what seems like so long.

It was a tough run and I ran as much as I walked. It
was the recovery that was so very tough. I had less
trouble keeping running than I did catching my breath.
It was a huge step for me and I will run again. I
will probably and almost certainly go for a run this
Thursday, either at lunch or after work.

I ran my usual route. Straight down Burrard and then
taking a left and cutting down to Coal Harbour. On my
way back I walked up a long flight of stairs and then
back to the office. It wasn't easy but I did it as I
walked and ran for about 40 minutes from the office to
the start of Stanley Park.

I have been struggling a great deal in the last two
weeks. Missing Michael terribly and dreaming about
him almost nightly. Some days I remember snippets of

dreams and other days I only know that he was there but I don't remember any details. I remember having my arms around his waist and sitting behind him. In the dreams he does not have any oxygen tubes and breathes well and on his own.

Christmas is tough too, but I have been cooking for the boys and spending lots of time with them. I have also been baking as well and not doing too much more than that. Errands mostly involve the boys or groceries. Virtually no clothes shopping in the past 2 to 3 weeks as I am watching my spending and I also know I shouldn't be shopping when I have a closet full of clothes. Ugh, they just don't fit.

We also have Kalea now, a second cat from the SPCA. She only moved in on Sunday, November 30th. She looks familiar to me. I don't know if she reminds me of Spyder, but I adore her already. I just want Mercury our other cat to tolerate her.

Her name means joy and happiness in Hawaiian. I chose a Hawaiian name because Michael and I loved Hawaii so very much. Also because their alphabet has 13 letters and 13 was always lucky for us. It was on the 13th hole that Michael proposed to me.

> *I miss you so much honey. I don't yearn for you as much, as I know yearning won't bring you back. I just started recently to remind myself that life is short and before I know it I will be with you again. I will work on my health though as I need to be fit, healthy and strong. I don't want diabetes, cancer, incontinence, high blood pressure, high cholesterol or anything else.*

From: Mae
To: Cynda
Date: Sunday, December 21, 2008 8:39 PM
Subject: A wish

Cynda

Dick & I wish you and the boys a very Merry Christmas
andf a Hsppy and a healthy New Year.
Our long period of silence has helped Dick & I through our
sorrow, we do not want you to think that we have been
ignoring you or that we have not thought about you.

Both Dick & I will always be eternally gratrefull for
Kindness and the patience you showered on Michael to
make his last days bearable.
We have yet to hear the disk that Michael made for us. I
am sure if I did, I would retreat into my shell again. It has
indeed been a rough period of our lives and I am sure you
are in the same position, but I do know as time passes-----
--time is a great healer.
Come to visit anytime you wish, you are very welcome.

Again take care and be happy. Mae & Dick

From: Cynda
To: Mae
Date: Tuesday, December 23, 2008 9:46 PM
Subject: A wish

Dear Mae and Dick:
Thank you for writing. I am touched by your note and really
appreciate you sharing how you feel. It means a lot.
The time and distance has helped me as well.
The past 4 1/2 months has been the toughest time in
my life. My whole life I always felt a void and when I met
Michael he made me whole. Learning to live without him

has been extremely painful and I am fortunate to have so many wonderful and poignant memories of the time we shared. I will be forever grateful that we found each other. I have thought of you often and more so of late with the holidays. I do want to see both of you very much and will call in the next day or so. Weather permitting we would like to drop by for a visit. We have plans to be in Vancouver tomorrow and on Christmas Day.

Merry Christmas and Happy New Year and the best for 2009.

Love,

Cynda

December 25, 2008

We spent Christmas Eve at Mary Anne's with Alexandra, Eric, Asia, and several other friends. It was really nice as I hadn't seen everyone in quite some time. There were lots of hugs and warm wishes.

I gave Christmas cards to everyone and wrote a great deal about how I felt and thanked everyone. I told both Alexandra and Eric just how proud their dad was of them. I told Eric that I saw how he grew in the 1½ years and how much I appreciated his help and that he stepped up when he was so needed. I told Alexandra how much it meant that she called him from Europe when he was in the hospice and how happy it made him.

I dreamt about Michael last night. I was back in that big old house that I dream about. I was lying in the bottom of a bunk bed with Michael and I could feel how thin he had become. I could feel his ribs. I remember feeling him and holding him tightly. He was cold and I was putting more blankets on him. I also dreamed about cantaloupe and cutting lots of up for breakfast. He wanted me to pack some for us for our trip so we could eat it in the car. It was really poignant to dream about him and more so to remember.

January 5, 2009

I was waiting at the bus stop to go to work in the early am and watching cars as they went by. A dark vehicle that looked like a Sunfire drove by. The window was rolled down all the way. I got a pretty good look and I swear it was Michael. Wearing the same Palm Springs baseball cap with the same profile that he had when we were in the Dominican but looking a bit better. He was wearing a dark top as well.

A co-worker said that it was because Michael was really with me and it was his way of showing me that he was here.

January 17, 2009

I had spent the night at my sister Abby's house and had a 35 minute run on her treadmill. I worked up a dripping wet sweat so it was really good. Later, Abby dropped me off at the bus loop and I headed home.

I did a few things around the house and after lunch decided to take a nap. I slept nearly upright in the corner of the living room sofa and I was a very comfortable. I was quite tired and slept very heavily. It was the type of heavy sleep where you hear what is going on around you, but it is so deep you cannot wake up or speak. I was in this state when I felt arms on either side of me from behind, pulling me up to support me. The arms were very warm and very strong. I felt very safe and secure. I was convinced that it was Michael. He was holding me and telling me that he was here to support me. It made me feel very safe and the experience was intense. Shortly after that I woke up. I had never before or since experienced anything like this.

March 18, 2009

It was a Thursday evening, probably March 5th. I was crying and reading a book written by a Medium about the dead and how they need to be remembered and loved. They like it when there are pictures of them recording their lives and when people talk about them. They just want to be remembered and loved. That night a dried hydrangea which normally sat in a vase moved from the nightstand to the middle of my desk. No cat could have done that and I know I didn't.

Another night after that happened the lid to my white cream coloured box was opened half way and the duck that used to lay on our bed at Michael's was lying on her side.

My bedroom lights flicker all the time and then settle down. No other lights in the house flicker. Coins get moved around on the dresser table at his brother's house.

I still dream about him often and in great detail.

From: Cynda
To: Michael
Date: Sunday, April 12, 2009 9:33 PM
Subject: Hi Honey

It's Easter Sunday and I miss you so very much.
I wish that I you could email me back a response. ...
I love you so much. I know that I am not ready to join you

*but today I wondered. I wanted to die so badly. I just wanted
to be dead as I couldn't hack it any more. I know you would
be so very mad at me for even thinking this way.*
*My only explanation is that I was just too overwhelmed with
sadness and maybe should have planned something for
today although I didn't want to as I had so many chores to
tend to in the house. I have at least accomplished all that I
set out to do and so in that respect I feel much better.*
*Maybe what I need is to talk to you this way often. It may
be just what I need. To talk to you.*
*I found the email you sent me back in November in giant
font telling me how you were just goofing around and that
you always love me.*
*I lost it last night when I touched your hat. It was the one
that Baree and Molly gave to you for Cuba. I love you in
that hat and I still remember so clearly when it flew off your
head at the lake.*

Sweet dreams my love
Honey Pot Pie

July 5, 2009

It has been many months since I have written and since
that time much has happened. I was lucky enough to be
chosen as a participant for the contest with the free
local newspaper. I have managed to get my health on
track after completing three months of boot camp. I
have lost 43 lbs and practice Pilates, Yoga, and climb
the Grouse Grind. I am not running lately because I
am grinding instead. Another connection, my boot camp
trainer turned out to be a second cousin of Molly's. I
was allowed to choose the boot camp location. We never
found out about the connection until later when I was
speaking to Molly's parents.

I have actually been coping better up until June 23rd. Then it all hit me way too hard. Coping has been overwhelming of late. Before that I had many days of happiness and fond happy memories of my life with you. I savored all the time we had together instead of missing and crying for you constantly which is what I am doing now.

I was on vacation this past week and it has been a real struggle. I remember too much of what and where I was a year ago. I miss you terribly and when I have tried not to cry over the course of the last several days, I find I am emotionally eating. I gained 6 lbs while on vacation. Not a good thing and good that I am back at work and back to my routine tomorrow. I am struggling and I feel broken and shattered. I returned a call to your Mom tonight and they were not home. Your voice came on with the answering machine and I burst into tears. I couldn't help but bawl when I hear you. I miss you so very much and get scared that I won't be with you one day. It horrifies me to think of not being with you again one day. I cannot survive if I think that way. Things were not perfect but you were everything I ever wanted. I know that although you were one of a kind there are others like you on PlentyOfFish. Guys in your age range who golf, fish and camp. Asian men named Michael or something else. None are you. I look in hopes that I find you there.

There is much to be grateful and happy for as I now have a beautiful deck in my backyard. It is fully fenced and I have a beautiful patio set as well. I also now have a meditation room. I worked very hard to make it all that I hoped it would be and I am very pleased with the end product.

I can't help but be sad right now as I guess I am anticipating how I will feel when it is the one year anniversary. I cannot even believe you have been gone from me for this long and yet I continue to breathe without you in my life.

CHAPTER EIGHTEEN
ONE YEAR LATER

August 10, 2009

It is the anniversary of Michael's death.

This morning I put Michael's stuffed bear and my duck on my bed. They used to be on the bed at home with Michael. We used to put bear and duck in compromising positions and we had lots of fun with that. It wasn't until today that I was okay with putting them on the bed again.

I wasn't feeling so well and I am sure it was because of the day. My head really hurt much of the day. I didn't cry much in the few days leading up and felt kind of weird and numb. I notice that when I don't cry I feel physically unwell or I end up stress eating.

I invited Michael's family to my place for dinner to celebrate his life. Everyone came.

Eric picked up a tri tip roast from Windsor Meats which we barbequed. It was a really nice evening and everyone had a nice time. Mary Anne and the boys didn't leave until 10 pm and I am so glad that we got together. It meant a lot to me to do that.

> Grief never ends....But it
> changes. It's a passage, not a
> place to stay. Grief is not a
> sign of weakness, nor a lack of
> faith...It is the price of love.
> Author unknown

October 1, 2009

I saw a rheumatologist that my family doctor sent me to earlier. This was a follow up visit with respect to the blisters I had on my lower left leg. I had not developed any new ones and these have still not healed completely.

December 9, 2009

Today was a turning point day for me. I had decided a few weeks ago that I would like to attend the Salvation Army Rotary Hospice's Christmas Memorial Service. I received an invite last year and did mention it to some of Michael's family members. I cannot even remember who, and we were all much too raw with pain to think of going. This year though, I really wanted to go; I wanted to be in the place where Michael spent his last days on this earth. Where there was so much love and compassion and caring for the human spirit. He wasn't at the hospice that long and so we never really interacted with other families but we did have much interaction with the staff and they were amazing. After he died, I sent them a thank you card along with a picture of Michael.

I wanted to go and decided not to let anyone know I was going. It was something just for me. I guess in a way it was a step towards healing. I met people I did not know from when Michael was a resident. I met the head volunteer, Jennifer as well as another volunteer. I told Jennifer that I hope to be a volunteer one day, when I don't cry all the time. I also told her that I want to help their hospice because this would be meaningful to me.

I spoke to one of the nurses who was there when Michael was and I felt bad because I didn't remember her. I remembered Major Abigail as well as the Chaplin Edward. We were gathered in the sanctuary and there was a choir made up of members of a local Chinese Alliance Church. I sat next to three Chinese sisters who had lost their Mom. One lady had lost her good friend who had been at the hospice for some nine months. Michael's stay was relatively short compared to others. I said that he had been in palliative care then he came home and I took care of him and then he moved into the hospice and so did I, as well as our cat Spyder. I shared that Spyder spent his time escaping from Michael's room then darting into the neighbor's and out his patio door only to be found slinking along the side of the building outside.

Michael's name was called out first and Edward said a few words and introduced me as Michael's fiancé. I guess the fact that I was his fiancé makes our love so much more tragic as we never got to marry. He also said that Michael was quite young. I wish there was more that he could have said but he had very little history as I guess we weren't there very long and kept to ourselves as there was a lot of family and friends coming and going. Many of the congregation shook my hand and gave me hugs. I thanked them for coming and singing for us. I was sobbing uncontrollably. I was such a cry baby. I went to the front with a lady from the Hospice and then on my way back to my seat Edward gave me a hug. I never expected to fall apart so badly. I remembered how Michael and I were in the sanctuary at the piano and he was teaching me to play chopsticks just a few days before he died. It was surreal to be back here and I remembered everything. I couldn't go to his room which was 111 as there was a patient there. It was just a room after all.

There were Christmas songs sung by the choir along with the group. We all received roses, yellow for men who had died and white for women. These roses were handed to family members to insert into a vase to form a bouquet. At the end of the evening we got our roses back. (I was so very lucky as I lost mine in the cab that I took from the hospice to the Skytrain. The very kind cab driver ran all the way up the escalator to bring my rose to me. I was distracted as I had been on the phone with a friend.)

I thanked Edward and Abigail as well as Francine for all their care and that they made everything so much easier.

Even though I cried a lot, it was good to come there. It gave me some peace in a way, if that makes any sense. I have only been to Richmond three times and each time it was for the airport. I had never gone back to the hospice after Michael died.

December 12, 2009

I had a dream very early this morning. It was so very real that I was certain it was happening as I was dreaming it. I was travelling locally on a Skytrain. I can only guess that it was the Canada Line as it was a different Skytrain and the scenery was different. I got off at a stop and walked up a hill and there was a beautiful Chinese garden. The ground was all covered in bark mulch and there were lots of Chinese statues and they were all gold in colour as well as I remember lots of red. I said out loud wow this is beautiful I need to show this to Andrew's dad and maybe we can do this on Christmas day. I have dreamed of this similar cul-de-sac before. It is always at the top of a street in the far left corner and I have no idea where it is but it feels familiar. I think my Mom was walking around there too.

Anyways, I quickly ran back down as I realize that I got off the Skytrain too soon and had to go further still. After this the memory of the dream is vague. I then dream of talking to Jeremy and using my cell and I called Michael and he answered the phone and it sounded just like him, just like how he used to sound. All I could think of was oh my God why haven't I called him sooner. What the hell was I thinking? How could I have moved out and then not gone to see him again. I was distraught and panicked in my dream and all I could think of was I have to get to him now and what was I thinking. I struggled to find his phone numbers as they were not in my cell and I remember thinking he will be so upset that I don't have his home or cell numbers in my phone and why hadn't I put them in there in the first place.

When I was on my way to Michael, he called me on the cell and asked me how long it would be before I would get there and I told him half an hour. He was going to get something to eat and the conversation was kind of garbled from his end as well. It was confusing and thoughts went through my head. How could I have left him alone and what did he look like now? I never got to see him in my dream and wished why didn't I go by the apartment when I was just in Richmond. I just kept thinking how could I have left him so alone. The dream ended when I woke up to my home phone ringing and my Blackberry vibrating.

It was four days after this dream that I finally read a letter that Michael had written to my eldest son Andrew back in March 2008. He wanted me to read it when he wrote it and I told him that I didn't need to as it was between the two of them. Now, so long after he died, it was like finding a piece of treasure.

I was really anxious about reading it. Part of me was worried I would be upset and possibly angry. After reading the letter I sobbed and couldn't stop for the longest time. Michael really loved me a lot, had my back and really cared about my sons and me so much. Here is an excerpt of the letter:

> "I'm sorry for getting between you and your Mom the other evening, but I had just enough of hearing the continued harassment you give your mother. Sons don't criticize and harass their parents as I see you do. They respect and appreciate them for what they have done to help you along in this world. Don't forget the other halves left your Mom and you two sons to fend without them . . . what if your Mom had decided not to take care of you guys! Don't ever think your Mom has had it easy. Do you really take stock of what she does to keep it all afloat for her and her sons?
>
> ...

Stop harassing your Mom and adjudicating her actions,
she is a grown woman who decides for herself what she
wants to do …. Not what you want her to do. A good
relationship with your Mom and only brother is a loving,
understanding one.

…

Please understand your Mom is an emotional person
and understanding of the situation coming at hand
would be big from her eldest. Your younger brother
fully comprehends the situation, believe it or not, she
certainly doesn't think you do or you've failed to let her
know. Please work on making it easy for your Mom to
talk with you without conflict and stress. Your Mom is a
very brave woman which I am so proud of. I am certain
she will find strength amongst the ashes."

Because it must be said, Andrew is an amazing, caring and loving man
and has been for several years now. I could not be prouder of the man
he has become. Michael was in our lives when Andrew was young, very
angry and trying to find his way in life. As well, Andrew and Michael had
similar personality traits. When Michael's mom met Andrew and heard
about him she understood why I was able to understand Michael so well.
Andrew was also very concerned about my well being as Michael was
very sick and likely to die.

CHAPTER NINETEEN
TWO YEARS LATER

August 10, 2010

On the second anniversary of Michael's death I was in Paris. It was my first time in Europe, and another bucket list item checked off. I wrote my first travel blog on Travellerspoint for this trip and here is an excerpt from that day:

> "I wanted to eat something special today. It has now been two years since my Michael passed away and Risotto was a favourite of both of ours. He made me amazing homemade risotto on a few occasions. We also sometimes ate it in restaurants. Margy and I toasted him with our wine and it all felt good. I wasn't so sad. I was in Paris after all and how could one be sad in the city of love. I had really been loved and for that I am blessed."

My blog is at http://sydney324.travellerspoint.com/toc/

More health problems loomed for me. Earlier in the year I had a routine fitness assessment at my gym, Bentall Centre Athletic Club. The trainer told me that my heartbeat did not sound right and that I should consult my family doctor. I had been having some problems with exercise for the past few months. I found myself to be extremely tired, winded, and had trouble finishing the Grouse Grind. It was never easy, but now it was taking an inordinate amount of time for me to complete.

Shortly after my return to Vancouver I attended the offices of a Cardiologist for a scheduled appointment. He diagnosed me with atrial fibrillation [a type of heart arrhythmia]. I had not previously had any heart problems. The condition was resolved with a course of medication over the next several months and my heart returned to normal sinus rhythm in early 2011. I no longer needed any medication except for a daily low dose of aspirin.

CHAPTER TWENTY
THREE YEARS LATER

August 10, 2011

On social media I posted the following message:

> *Three years ago today my heart shattered. Miss you so*
> *much that some days I can't believe I didn't die from the*
> *immense pain. Am healing and sometimes life sucks. I am*
> *looking at the positive side as I know I am blessed. I miss*
> *your love, laughter and passion for life. There is much to*
> *be grateful for. I know I will see you when I get to the other*
> *side when it's my time. Miss u BF. Love HP.*

September 19, 2011

It was just over a week past the second anniversary of Matt's Dad's passing and he was so kind to email me this.

> *Cynda,*
> *Thanks! I've been thinking of you and what a gift it was for*
> *Michael to have you.*
> *Lots of love, Matt*

March 26, 2012

It had been five years since I had been to Cuba with Michael. I had always wanted to return and now I was here again with Jeremy.

I wrote the following in my journal:

> Today was an emotional day. Monday, March 26th would have been Michael's 58th birthday. Being here on his birthday meant the world to me. We were so newly in love when we came five years ago. I had always wanted to return. I just never knew if I would get the chance to. Life sometimes gets in the way and your best laid plans never come to fruition. Blessed and grateful is how I feel to be here now.
>
> Back in 2007 we arrived on Michael's birthday. When the plane landed he burst into tears. He never expected to see this birthday and was so overjoyed.
>
> Sharing the trip with Jeremy is that much more special. He's a gentle soul and worries about mom.
>
> Today I set my alarm and woke up at 8 am. Off for a run. Originally I was going to the gym but then I spotted two runners and I was so excited. I like to always run whenever I am on vacation. I never ran in Cuba last time as the prospect made Michael nervous and I was also uneasy. It was after all a communist country with machine guns, why would you run unless you are in trouble.

Remembering: Cynda Yeasting took her *Burnaby NOW* along on a special trip to Cuba from March 24 to April 1 with her youngest son, Jeremy. Her first trip to Cuba was five years ago with her fiancé, Michael, who died of cancer in August 2008. This trip took place on what would have been his 58th birthday on March 26, and Cynda wanted to celebrate and honour his life. Here she is in front of the famous Ambos Mundos hotel in Old Havana, where Ernest Hemingway lived for seven years and wrote his novel *For Whom the Bell Tolls.*

Burnaby Now Paper Postcards

Later that year I was a volunteer crew member with the BC Cancer Foundation at the Ride to Conquer Cancer. It was also Alexandra's first time as a participant and I got to see her cross the finish line. It was a bittersweet moment.

Our participation made a difference in the fight to conquer cancer. Cancer can make you feel so helpless. Being a volunteer gave me a voice as I was actively doing something to fight cancer. It was an amazing experience and I volunteered again in 2013.

As a volunteer, my job was simple, I handed out snacks, filled water bottles, talked to and cheered on riders. I knew many of the riders and it was truly an empowering event.

CHAPTER TWENTY-ONE
FOUR YEARS LATER

August 10, 2012

On social media I posted the following message:

> Michael Chu. Today is 4 years since you left your earthly body. I am doing my best to fulfill the promise you had me make to you... To Be Happy. Loving my fitness and embracing the joy of living and breathing.
>
> I'm gonna be one hot, yoga stretching, tree hugging, grinding, smiling, free spirited woman!!! Whoops already am.
>
> I have grown because of you.

I had climbed the Grouse Grind that morning for the ninth time that year.

This was a very busy and life changing year for me. My home was up for sale and I would be moving back to the West End, where I grew up. This was another bucket list item for me.

The year had been one of letting go of much of what I no longer needed, lots of exercise, spending time with friends, family and soaking up the outdoors. I was healing and life was amazing.

CHAPTER TWENTY-TWO
FIVE YEARS LATER

July 6, 2013

Today I was fortunate enough to check off another bucket list item. I was travelling to Cambodia with a group of volunteers from across Canada. I had volunteered with HOPE International Development Agency to work and live alongside communities without running water or electricity. We would be learning about the day to day challenges of life in a developing country and how the lives of these families were being transformed.

It was a life changing trip and I documented my experience. My blog is at http://cyndacambodia2013.travellerspoint.com/toc/

For information on HOPE International Development Agency go to http://www.hope-international.com/index.php

August 9, 2013

On social media I posted the following message:

Dear Michael. Tomorrow it will be 5 years since you passed away. Hard to believe so much time has gone by.

It has taken a long time but I am mostly happy these days honey. You made me promise you that I would be happy and it has been a long tough road back to joy and with each year I feel less sad. I will always miss you and you will always be a part of my heart.

When I told a friend that I was feeling a bit out of sorts because I was not sadder and that it feels like you are fading from my memory and I feel bad she responded with "It's not that he's fading from your memory, it's simply that you have come to be at peace with his passing and have finally taken all those memories, good, bad, heartwarming, and integrated them into the fabric of your everyday life...that's why it feels less "special"...because it's woven into the fabric of your life and routines...

CHAPTER TWENTY-THREE
SIX YEARS LATER

August 10, 2014

On social media I posted the following message:

Dear Michael.

Six years ago today, late in the morning you quietly took your last breath and slipped out of our lives. It was a Sunday then and sometimes it feels like it was just yesterday.

My life with you seems so foreign at times yet so very familiar and if I allow myself to miss you too much the ache in me is just too much to take. My physical body hurts and I know I have slowly built a new life that you are not part of.

Moving on....two steps forward and one back...I am a work in progress. I still love you and I guess I always will and it is hard. This year feels harder yet life has more joy than ever before. Maybe it is because you aren't here to share it with me.

This year was a very different day as I was at a wedding and it was a day filled with love and great joy.

CHAPTER TWENTY-FOUR
LIFE LATELY

January 12, 2015

Yesterday, it was eight years ago that I first spoke to Michael on the phone. I cannot believe that so much time has passed and so very quickly.

The last several months have been most difficult. The atrial fibrillation that had first occurred in 2010 returned unexpectedly in early October. During the 3½ year absence I was able to boot camp, spin, run, practice hot yoga, hike and snowshoe without any problems. I have been on sick leave from my job since early November.

My tabby Chesney who was only five years old, fell ill late November and after numerous procedures and surgery, I had to make the difficult decision to have him euthanized. The fact that Chesney was terminal was like dealing with Michael's cancer. Michael greatly admired the country singer Kenny Chesney and that is how Chesney got his name. I believe that losing Chesney was another life lesson for me. As hard as it was to lose Michael I know that it was his time, just as it was Chesney's time. Death is a natural part of

life. If we did not have death, we would not appreciate life as much.

It is a cathartic release to finally finish writing our
story. As I read and edit various sections of the
book, I am taken back to those times and my heart
aches. Crying is a frequent occurrence and I often
have to step away and take a breather. I am surprised
as to how much it still hurts, but the pain has definitely softened, and there are so many good memories
that bring comfort.

My hope is that our story will be a comfort to those
diagnosed with cancer and their loved ones. It is
my wish to raise a large amount of money for the
BC Cancer Foundation and other Cancer organizations
around the world from partial proceeds of the sales of
this book.

January 20, 2015

Today it is eight years ago that I first went on a
date with Michael. Life still has its difficulties of
course, but I have grown a great deal since his death.
I have gotten to know myself and I do my best to never
take life for granted. I was so lucky to have found
him. Our time together wasn't long but we managed to
squeeze in a lifetime of love, laughter and tears.
When I have a tough time missing him it is because I
miss his love. I was so very loved and I know this
not because he always told me, but because I always
felt it.

CHAPTER TWENTY-FIVE
DEFINITELY NOT THE END

Grief is a funny thing. Somehow, society expects you to get over losing someone, but you never get over the loss, you just learn to continue living without them. They loved you and just wanted the best for you. You honour them by living your life to the fullest, no matter how hard it might be at times. Michael would not have wanted me to waste my life by moping or being sad.

I have times when I am so consumed by grief that it is like he just died. Fortunately these occurrences are shorter and less frequent as the years go by. The pain of the loss is at times so unbelievably intense. I miss him most when I am scared and I have been scared a lot in the past nine months.

With the health issues that I am currently dealing with, my heart is constantly in the forefront. It is the only organ in your body that has to work 24/7. Even your brain gets a break when you sleep. I am grateful that my heart beats and is constantly emotional. It is the emotions that make me feel most alive. I never want to lose that.

I am grateful for my heart's resilience, physically of late, as well as emotionally over the years, and more so in the last eight years. I will always miss you my dearest Flet, Michael Chu.

Since Michael's death life has been a matter of three steps forward and two back but I strive to keep looking ahead. There is much on my bucket list and life is too short to be scared. Michael reminded me to be brave and courageous.

Although it is natural to have heartache and loss in life, I strive to focus on the immense joys my heart has had. Time does help heal and lessen the pain. I feel much gratitude to wake up each day.

I will always be a work in progress but I know that I am okay and I am better for having been with Michael. We had quality and not quantity; this was a phrase that he repeated often.

What Cancer Cannot Do

Cancer is so limited...
It cannot cripple love.
It cannot shatter hope.
It cannot corrode faith.
It cannot eat away peace.
It cannot destroy confidence.
It cannot kill friendship.
It cannot shut out memories.
It cannot silence courage.
It cannot reduce eternal life.
It cannot quench the spirit.

Author Unknown

APPENDIX A

Here is my eulogy:

Michael - Celebration of Life

Hi, I'm Cynda, Michael's fiancé.

Thanks to William and Sally for letting us Celebrate Michael's life here. Mary Anne, I, Matt and William wanted to do something to honour and remember Michael. I know Michael would have been pleased and really pissed to have missed out on the food.

My story comes in two parts and it's Side B first.

I want to share an excerpt of an email which I sent to some friends and family. My apologies to those that have already heard it but I have also altered it some. What I wrote means a great deal to me and so here it is…

'Tears wash away the pain leaving only strength, so cry today, so you can stand tall tomorrow.' (My younger son, Jeremy read this somewhere.)

My world, as I know it, ended on Sunday, August 10th, around 11:30 am.

That's when my dear sweet, bossy and adorable Michael took his last breath at the Salvation Army Rotary Hospice in Richmond, BC.

He died peacefully surrounded by loved ones. Although he wasn't able to speak or respond to us after 3:00 am Sunday we continued to talk to him.

Prior to that on Saturday, despite breathing distress, he was able to talk to us although it was at times laboured and difficult. He told us that he couldn't go on any more. He asked me to call his family and get them to come right away.

On that day we talked about life and death. It was all peaceful and Michael seemed to be satisfied with our talk. He had all three meals that day and those that knew Michael knew how much he loved to eat. I would joke that those that Michael loves get fatter, even Spyder our cat gained weight. Michael's terms of endearment for me were Honey, Honey Pot Pie and Sweetie Pie. You get the drift.

He was the smartest, most charming and interesting man I have ever met in my life. He gave me many gifts that I will treasure forever. He taught me how to love again and to trust. I am a much better cook because of Michael and I even learned how to play chopsticks on the piano with him about 3 weeks ago.

Because the enjoyment of food was an important part of our relationship, Michael and I ended up reviewing restaurants at www.dinehere.ca. His reviewer name is Hargow and mine Dawntart. For those who don't know, Hargow is a shrimp dumpling and Dawn Tart spelled don tart is a dessert. There is another reviewer named Chaisubow which is BBQ Pork Bun.

Although we had only been together for just under 1 year and 7 months we lived a lifetime. We were soul mates and few are lucky enough to ever find that.

He gave me a great deal of happiness and although his illness caused us both great sorrow, I am so grateful that when I found him that he chose me too.

He had a very kind and gentle and caring side and I was the lucky beneficiary of all of this. He would always tell me how much he loved me and tell me in great detail. Our life together wasn't long but we filled it with more love and life than others have in the space of 30 years.

Some people come into our lives, leave footprints on our heart, and we are never, ever the same...

Now for Side A of my story. This one is a happy story.

I want to tell you how I met Michael. A co-worker had recommended a dating website aptly called "PlentyOfFish". Michael's name was "Fred Flounder."

I hadn't dated in over 8 years as I was busy raising children and had no time or energy for a partner. I dated a few guys before I met Michael and my goal was to find a really special man. I told Michael I didn't want mediocre, otherwise, why bother.

Michael's tag line said "It's the Best Time of My Life"

His profession was "Enjoying Life"

His interests were "outdoor walks, travelling, Kenny Chesney, golf, dining, photography, fishing, music and biking."

Under About Me it said "I am new to this site and would love to find the woman I've been looking for all my life, my best friend and lover. I am 2nd generation Canadian with lots of British Columbian family history. I was born, raised and lived here all my life. I am warm and caring, a listener and look younger than my 52 yrs. I worked in the healthcare profession with the disabled and geriatric populations. I now live alone and have 2 grown kids. I love to cook and share meals with my family and friends, or just spend time hangin at home. I'm an avid outdoors person, and a lifetime golfer. I love to fish and find myself in idyllic settings on our beautiful BC rivers or at our lake in the Cariboo. I play and listen to music and really enjoy travel. You are a non smoker, honest, sincere, warm and caring with very insignificant issues. I spend my time cherishing every minute of my life, appreciating it's challenges and try to live it to the max as we only have one crack at it. I hope you feel the same. Petite would be nice. I do have time to spend with you."

Under the first date section he wrote "coffee, lunch, walk in the park or along the beach, a bucket of balls, or what you may have in mind, something to get to know who you are."

My tag line said "Passionate about life"

My interests were "running, shopping (I never misled him), yoga, theatre, movies, community events"

Under About Me it said "I have been a single parent for 14 years. I have an adult son and a teenaged son. I run, practice yoga, and love the Grouse Grind. I enjoy and love the outdoors and nature. Walks or runs through Stanley Park make me smile. I also enjoy going out for dinner, movies, occasional theatre or concerts. Just hanging out. I care about making a difference. I fundraise for a few causes that are important to me. I am social but I also enjoy and am comfortable having alone time. I joke that I am part Crow as I am easily distracted by something that sparkles. My life is happy but I am at the point where I am wanting to find someone special to share it with. I know who I am and what I want. I am emotionally and financially stable. I am looking for a like minded person. Someone who wants to make a difference in life. Someone who wants to be healthy and fit or is striving to be. We all had to start somewhere. I don't play head games, life is too short for that. I want someone who is honest, has integrity, is sincere and most of all, down to earth.

Under the first date section I wrote "A first meeting could be a walk in the park, literally, Stanley Park or English Bay, a couple of cups of coffee or tea. Just some light, get to know you conversation, or perhaps something more challenging?"

I emailed Michael. He emailed back with his phone numbers and told me that he was a bit of a nitehawk so don't worry if its too late. I called him around 10 pm and we talked for over two hours. We would have probably talked all night except that I had to be up for work very early the next day. He was charming, candid and honest. He told me about his cancer right away, that it was stage 4 and that he was currently stable. I think I was smitten from that first call.

He told me that he was going to Palm Springs for a golf trip and would be back next Friday but that he really wanted to meet and would like to take me out to dinner on Saturday.

When he got back we talked and made dinner plans. He would come to pick me up and I gave him directions and a description of my place. Told him I was right behind the big tree. Well it definitely wasn't the best description as our complex is surrounded by lots of big trees. By the way for those that know Michael, he was also about 15 mins late for our first date.

Anyways when I laid eyes on him he looked as adorable as I expected. That never changed for me. I often told him that I adored him even when he was Mr. Crankypants.

Michael never wanted a funeral. He said he wasn't that kind of guy. He didn't want everyone to be weeping and sad. But he was fine with a dinner. He knew better than anyone just how important it was to savour all of life and so he doesn't want any of us to waste life by being too sad.

We are having this Celebration of Life today to share our stories, to laugh, grieve, cry and honour Michael. He was one hell of a special man and we will all miss him.

I heard a line a few days ago and it goes like this. Just because you are sick it doesn't mean that you don't get a life. That really summed up Michael's attitude. He really knew how to live and that is his lesson for all of us.

So make him happy, I know he is watching and with us.

Thanks for listening.